Gateways to Change

Gateways to Change

Gloria Gray and Jenni Sinclair

Writer's Showcase
New York   Lincoln   Shanghai

Gateways to Change

Writer's Showcase
an imprint of iUniverse, Inc.

For information address:
iUniverse
2021 Pine Lake Road, Suite 100
Lincoln, NE 68512
www.iuniverse.com

ISBN: 0-595-24869-1

Printed in the United States of America

Dedication

This book is dedicated to my beautiful daughter, Trina Marie, and my soul mate Kenneth Riley. They are free spirits who taught me the lesson of unconditional love. Also, I want to express my special thanks to Jenni Sinclair and her husband Don. Jenni remains my life-long friend and co-creator.

All their love contains no boundaries and even though we are apart, their presence still embraces me. May their inner glow always light their passageways, so even miles disappear. Together we all share bonds that we can't explain. I thank God for sending them my way. May I hold them forever near.

Gloria Gray—July 2002

This book is dedicated to my husband, Don Sinclair, my true love and my best friend who loves me in spite of myself; to my mother, Berniece Bryant, who always reminded me to be patient, that God isn't finished with me yet; to my forever friend, Gloria Gray, for sharing this journey with me; and to my cherished clients, who have trusted me with their deepest, darkest secrets and shared with me their personal hopes, wishes, and dreams.

Jenni Sinclair—July 2002

Acknowledgments

I wish to express appreciation to my life-long friends, Mary Ann Kuwabara, always my harbor in a storm; Yvonne Davidson, always the honest and practical Virgo; and N.L. Cooke. Lovingly known as Dr. Capt. Cooke, this Capricorn taught me patience, the law of divine order and with healing hands often eased my physical pain. Joan Pipes, another Capricorn, remains a wonderful friend. She is always there to extend a life-line. All these steadfast astrological earth sign friends have kept me afloat and buoyed my spirit through the high and low tides of my life. Their emotional support and encouragement has always kept me focused toward the light.

My appreciation is also extended to Kenneth and Jim Bryant for their personal friendship over the years. And not to be forgotten is my journalism teacher, Wayne Field. This man made a profound difference in my life.

Ed Rhinehardt—Thank you for your editing assistance and honest critique. Your positive encouragement means so much.

I am truly blessed.

Gloria Gray—2002

Acknowledgments

No matter where our journey takes us, we are never alone. No matter what we do, we don't do it by ourselves. This book is no exception. I have been blessed my entire life with family and friends who have taken the time to truly get to know me and to love me as much as I love them.

I thank my husband, Don, for his patience and unconditional love, for the shared respect he has for my career and my clients, and for his honest critique of this book. I give thanks to my sister, Carol, whose constant love and endless energy is an inspiration—especially after all she has gone through. To my brother, Ken, for his sense of humor and for being a constant reminder that we always land on our feet. And to my brother, Jim, whose inner child and gift of gab provide endless entertainment for us all.

Thanks also to my friends Sue Tippett and Laura Kaiser for their friendship and encouragement, and for their honest critique in reviewing this book.

I thank God, my Angels and Guides—for all that has been and for all that will be—THANKS!

Jenni Sinclair—2002

Contents
Your Itinerary

List of Tables

Introduction

In your hands you hold a treasure chest. The key is in your mind and in your right of free choice and free will. The free will is to search within to find the gifts of knowledge that await you. Flow into that which beckons you.

Numbers affect our lives in endless ways. Through numerological analysis you can chart your course to fulfill your destiny. With it you get a crow's nest view of the challenges, wild storms, hidden dangers and safe ports on your personal voyage.

Find the charts calculated to your individual birth date. Each year, month and day briefly describes the point of significant promise. By sharing tools and techniques from the ancient arts of numerology and astrology, the authors hope to awaken each reader to valuable insights to help deal with everyday life. You may be surprised to discover and confirm how much you have already suspected through your own intuition.

Your daily life planner will become your personal captain's log of important developments in your life's journey. It is a fitting tool to all that seek knowledge in the spiritual sciences. The journey is your treasure.

Bon Voyage!

How To Use Your Planner
Navigate By Numbers

Waves run ahead of storms to cry their warning and to foretell its effect on human affairs. Warned by the approach of swells, ships can seek safety in port or in the open sea, and so can you.

All history involves people, places, trends and change. While the challenge of your destiny represents a life-long effort, there are cycles and sub-cycles of time that have more immediate effects in your daily life.

Your Planner Consists of 3 Parts

- PORTS OF CALL   (Your Personal Year)
- TREASURE MAPS   (Your Personal Months)
- DAILY COMPASS   (Your Personal Days)

Ports of Call

Lifetimes are mapped in nine-year cycles, measured by the universal vibrations for the numbers 1 to 9. Life is an ongoing journey and these cycles repeat throughout a lifetime. Everyone journeys through each recurring cycle to embark on experiences that will open new horizons of consciousness.

Your itinerary will take you through nine Ports of Call. These nine ports cover the entire spectrum of human experience. Use the charts calculated for your birth date to reveal the trend of your personal year for the purpose of helping you to become more aware of the ebb and flow of the universe and your place in it.

Treasure Maps

Like a treasure map, each monthly vibration provides pointers to fulfillment. It identifies and explains the focus that shapes each month by pointing out the experiences and the people you can expect to encounter.

Daily Compass

Keep alert to the trend of thoughts and actions each day suggests. Make better informed choices, exercising your free will and freedom of choice. Pay attention to change so you can ride the crest of the wave rather than the tail end.

Welcome Aboard!
Searchers—Seekers—Voyagers—All

Ports of Call
1 through 9

Yearly Influences

How to Find the Gateway
to Your Personal Port of Call

- Find your birthday on the gateway grid for the current year.

- Then turn to the matching synopsis to reveal the trend of your personal port of call.

Gateway Grid Example for												
March 7, 2003												
To find your personal Port of Call, go down to your Birth Day, then across to your Birth Month to find your Personal Port of Call for 2003.												
Day	Jan	Feb	**Mar**	Apr	May	Jun	Jul	Aug	Sep	Oct	Nov	Dec
1	7	8	9	1	2	3	4	5	6	7	8	9
2	8	9	1	2	3	4	5	6	7	8	9	1
3	9	1	2	3	4	5	6	7	8	9	1	2
4	1	2	3	4	5	6	7	8	9	1	2	3
5	2	3	4	5	6	7	8	9	1	2	3	4
6	3	4	5	6	7	8	9	1	2	3	4	5
7	4	5	**6**	7	8	9	1	2	3	4	5	6
8	5	6	7	8	9	1	2	3	4	5	6	7

Table 1. Port of Call Gateway for 2002

To find your personal Port of Call, go down to your Birth Day, then across to your Birth Month to find your Personal Port of Call for 2002.											
Day	Jan	Feb	Mar	Apr	May	Jun	Jul	Aug	Sep	Oct	Nov	Dec
1	6	7	8	9	1	2	3	4	5	6	7	8
2	7	8	9	1	2	3	4	5	6	7	8	9
3	8	9	1	2	3	4	5	6	7	8	9	1
4	9	1	2	3	4	5	6	7	8	9	1	2
5	1	2	3	4	5	6	7	8	9	1	2	3
6	2	3	4	5	6	7	8	9	1	2	3	4
7	3	4	5	6	7	8	9	1	2	3	4	5
8	4	5	6	7	8	9	1	2	3	4	5	6
9	5	6	7	8	9	1	2	3	4	5	6	7
10	6	7	8	9	1	2	3	4	5	6	7	8
11	7	8	9	1	2	3	4	5	6	7	8	9
12	8	9	1	2	3	4	5	6	7	8	9	1
13	9	1	2	3	4	5	6	7	8	9	1	2
14	1	2	3	4	5	6	7	8	9	1	2	3
15	2	3	4	5	6	7	8	9	1	2	3	4
16	3	4	5	6	7	8	9	1	2	3	4	5
17	4	5	6	7	8	9	1	2	3	4	5	6
18	5	6	7	8	9	1	2	3	4	5	6	7
19	6	7	8	9	1	2	3	4	5	6	7	8
20	7	8	9	1	2	3	4	5	6	7	8	9
21	8	9	1	2	3	4	5	6	7	8	9	1
22	9	1	2	3	4	5	6	7	8	9	1	2
23	1	2	3	4	5	6	7	8	9	1	2	3
24	2	3	4	5	6	7	8	9	1	2	3	4
25	3	4	5	6	7	8	9	1	2	3	4	5
26	4	5	6	7	8	9	1	2	3	4	5	6
27	5	6	7	8	9	1	2	3	4	5	6	7
28	6	7	8	9	1	2	3	4	5	6	7	8
29	7	8	9	1	2	3	4	5	6	7	8	9
30	8		1	2	3	4	5	6	7	8	9	1
31	9		2		4		6	7		9		2

Table 2. Port of Call Gateway for 2003

To find your personal Port of Call, go down to your Birth Day, then across to your Birth Month to find your Personal Port of Call for 2003.											
Day	Jan	Feb	Mar	Apr	May	Jun	Jul	Aug	Sep	Oct	Nov	Dec
1	7	8	9	1	2	3	4	5	6	7	8	9
2	8	9	1	2	3	4	5	6	7	8	9	1
3	9	1	2	3	4	5	6	7	8	9	1	2
4	1	2	3	4	5	6	7	8	9	1	2	3
5	2	3	4	5	6	7	8	9	1	2	3	4
6	3	4	5	6	7	8	9	1	2	3	4	5
7	4	5	6	7	8	9	1	2	3	4	5	6
8	5	6	7	8	9	1	2	3	4	5	6	7
9	6	7	8	9	1	2	3	4	5	6	7	8
10	7	8	9	1	2	3	4	5	6	7	8	9
11	8	9	1	2	3	4	5	6	7	8	9	1
12	9	1	2	3	4	5	6	7	8	9	1	2
13	1	2	3	4	5	6	7	8	9	1	2	3
14	2	3	4	5	6	7	8	9	1	2	3	4
15	3	4	5	6	7	8	9	1	2	3	4	5
16	4	5	6	7	8	9	1	2	3	4	5	6
17	5	6	7	8	9	1	2	3	4	5	6	7
18	6	7	8	9	1	2	3	4	5	6	7	8
19	7	8	9	1	2	3	4	5	6	7	8	9
20	8	9	1	2	3	4	5	6	7	8	9	1
21	9	1	2	3	4	5	6	7	8	9	1	2
22	1	2	3	4	5	6	7	8	9	1	2	3
23	2	3	4	5	6	7	8	9	1	2	3	4
24	3	4	5	6	7	8	9	1	2	3	4	5
25	4	5	6	7	8	9	1	2	3	4	5	6
26	5	6	7	8	9	1	2	3	4	5	6	7
27	6	7	8	9	1	2	3	4	5	6	7	8
28	7	8	9	1	2	3	4	5	6	7	8	9
29	8	9	1	2	3	4	5	6	7	8	9	1
30	9		2	3	4	5	6	7	8	9	1	2
31	1		3		5		7	8		1		3

Table 3. Port of Call Gateway for 2004

| To find your personal Port of Call, go down to your Birth Day, then across to your Birth Month to find your Personal Port of Call for 2004. | | | | | | | | | | | |
Day	Jan	Feb	Mar	Apr	May	Jun	Jul	Aug	Sep	Oct	Nov	Dec
1	8	9	1	2	3	4	5	6	7	8	9	1
2	9	1	2	3	4	5	6	7	8	9	1	2
3	1	2	3	4	5	6	7	8	9	1	2	3
4	2	3	4	5	6	7	8	9	1	2	3	4
5	3	4	5	6	7	8	9	1	2	3	4	5
6	4	5	6	7	8	9	1	2	3	4	5	6
7	5	6	7	8	9	1	2	3	4	5	6	7
8	6	7	8	9	1	2	3	4	5	6	7	8
9	7	8	9	1	2	3	4	5	6	7	8	9
10	8	9	1	2	3	4	5	6	7	8	9	1
11	9	1	2	3	4	5	6	7	8	9	1	2
12	1	2	3	4	5	6	7	8	9	1	2	3
13	2	3	4	5	6	7	8	9	1	2	3	4
14	3	4	5	6	7	8	9	1	2	3	4	5
15	4	5	6	7	8	9	1	2	3	4	5	6
16	5	6	7	8	9	1	2	3	4	5	6	7
17	6	7	8	9	1	2	3	4	5	6	7	8
18	7	8	9	1	2	3	4	5	6	7	8	9
19	8	9	1	2	3	4	5	6	7	8	9	1
20	9	1	2	3	4	5	6	7	8	9	1	2
21	1	2	3	4	5	6	7	8	9	1	2	3
22	2	3	4	5	6	7	8	9	1	2	3	4
23	3	4	5	6	7	8	9	1	2	3	4	5
24	4	5	6	7	8	9	1	2	3	4	5	6
25	5	6	7	8	9	1	2	3	4	5	6	7
26	6	7	8	9	1	2	3	4	5	6	7	8
27	7	8	9	1	2	3	4	5	6	7	8	9
28	8	9	1	2	3	4	5	6	7	8	9	1
29	9	1	2	3	4	5	6	7	8	9	1	2
30	1		3	4	5	6	7	8	9	1	2	3
31	2		4		6		8	9		2		4

Table 4. Port of Call Gateway for 2005

To find your personal Port of Call, go down to your Birth Day, then across to your Birth Month to find your Personal Port of Call for 2005.											
Day	Jan	Feb	Mar	Apr	May	Jun	Jul	Aug	Sep	Oct	Nov	Dec
1	9	1	2	3	4	5	6	7	8	9	1	2
2	1	2	3	4	5	6	7	8	9	1	2	3
3	2	3	4	5	6	7	8	9	1	2	3	4
4	3	4	5	6	7	8	9	1	2	3	4	5
5	4	5	6	7	8	9	1	2	3	4	5	6
6	5	6	7	8	9	1	2	3	4	5	6	7
7	6	7	8	9	1	2	3	4	5	6	7	8
8	7	8	9	1	2	3	4	5	6	7	8	9
9	8	9	1	2	3	4	5	6	7	8	9	1
10	9	1	2	3	4	5	6	7	8	9	1	2
11	1	2	3	4	5	6	7	8	9	1	2	3
12	2	3	4	5	6	7	8	9	1	2	3	4
13	3	4	5	6	7	8	9	1	2	3	4	5
14	4	5	6	7	8	9	1	2	3	4	5	6
15	5	6	7	8	9	1	2	3	4	5	6	7
16	6	7	8	9	1	2	3	4	5	6	7	8
17	7	8	9	1	2	3	4	5	6	7	8	9
18	8	9	1	2	3	4	5	6	7	8	9	1
19	9	1	2	3	4	5	6	7	8	9	1	2
20	1	2	3	4	5	6	7	8	9	1	2	3
21	2	3	4	5	6	7	8	9	1	2	3	4
22	3	4	5	6	7	8	9	1	2	3	4	5
23	4	5	6	7	8	9	1	2	3	4	5	6
24	5	6	7	8	9	1	2	3	4	5	6	7
25	6	7	8	9	1	2	3	4	5	6	7	8
26	7	8	9	1	2	3	4	5	6	7	8	9
27	8	9	1	2	3	4	5	6	7	8	9	1
28	9	1	2	3	4	5	6	7	8	9	1	2
29	1	2	3	4	5	6	7	8	9	1	2	3
30	2		4	5	6	7	8	9	1	2	3	4
31	3		5		7		9	1		3		5

Table 5. Port of Call Gateway for 2006

To find your personal Port of Call, go down to your Birth Day, then across to your Birth Month to find your Personal Port of Call for 2006.											
Day	Jan	Feb	Mar	Apr	May	Jun	Jul	Aug	Sep	Oct	Nov	Dec
1	1	2	3	4	5	6	7	8	9	1	2	3
2	2	3	4	5	6	7	8	9	1	2	3	4
3	3	4	5	6	7	8	9	1	2	3	4	5
4	4	5	6	7	8	9	1	2	3	4	5	6
5	5	6	7	8	9	1	2	3	4	5	6	7
6	6	7	8	9	1	2	3	4	5	6	7	8
7	7	8	9	1	2	3	4	5	6	7	8	9
8	8	9	1	2	3	4	5	6	7	8	9	1
9	9	1	2	3	4	5	6	7	8	9	1	2
10	1	2	3	4	5	6	7	8	9	1	2	3
11	2	3	4	5	6	7	8	9	1	2	3	4
12	3	4	5	6	7	8	9	1	2	3	4	5
13	4	5	6	7	8	9	1	2	3	4	5	6
14	5	6	7	8	9	1	2	3	4	5	6	7
15	6	7	8	9	1	2	3	4	5	6	7	8
16	7	8	9	1	2	3	4	5	6	7	8	9
17	8	9	1	2	3	4	5	6	7	8	9	1
18	9	1	2	3	4	5	6	7	8	9	1	2
19	1	2	3	4	5	6	7	8	9	1	2	3
20	2	3	4	5	6	7	8	9	1	2	3	4
21	3	4	5	6	7	8	9	1	2	3	4	5
22	4	5	6	7	8	9	1	2	3	4	5	6
23	5	6	7	8	9	1	2	3	4	5	6	7
24	6	7	8	9	1	2	3	4	5	6	7	8
25	7	8	9	1	2	3	4	5	6	7	8	9
26	8	9	1	2	3	4	5	6	7	8	9	1
27	9	1	2	3	4	5	6	7	8	9	1	2
28	1	2	3	4	5	6	7	8	9	1	2	3
29	2	3	4	5	6	7	8	9	1	2	3	4
30	3		5	6	7	8	9	1	2	3	4	5
31	4		6		8		1	2		4		6

Table 6. Port of Call Gateway for 2007

To find your personal Port of Call, go down to your Birth Day, then across to your Birth Month to find your Personal Port of Call for 2007.											
Day	Jan	Feb	Mar	Apr	May	Jun	Jul	Aug	Sep	Oct	Nov	Dec
1	2	3	4	5	6	7	8	9	1	2	3	4
2	3	4	5	6	7	8	9	1	2	3	4	5
3	4	5	6	7	8	9	1	2	3	4	5	6
4	5	6	7	8	9	1	2	3	4	5	6	7
5	6	7	8	9	1	2	3	4	5	6	7	8
6	7	8	9	1	2	3	4	5	6	7	8	9
7	8	9	1	2	3	4	5	6	7	8	9	1
8	9	1	2	3	4	5	6	7	8	9	1	2
9	1	2	3	4	5	6	7	8	9	1	2	3
10	2	3	4	5	6	7	8	9	1	2	3	4
11	3	4	5	6	7	8	9	1	2	3	4	5
12	4	5	6	7	8	9	1	2	3	4	5	6
13	5	6	7	8	9	1	2	3	4	5	6	7
14	6	7	8	9	1	2	3	4	5	6	7	8
15	7	8	9	1	2	3	4	5	6	7	8	9
16	8	9	1	2	3	4	5	6	7	8	9	1
17	9	1	2	3	4	5	6	7	8	9	1	2
18	1	2	3	4	5	6	7	8	9	1	2	3
19	2	3	4	5	6	7	8	9	1	2	3	4
20	3	4	5	6	7	8	9	1	2	3	4	5
21	4	5	6	7	8	9	1	2	3	4	5	6
22	5	6	7	8	9	1	2	3	4	5	6	7
23	6	7	8	9	1	2	3	4	5	6	7	8
24	7	8	9	1	2	3	4	5	6	7	8	9
25	8	9	1	2	3	4	5	6	7	8	9	1
26	9	1	2	3	4	5	6	7	8	9	1	2
27	1	2	3	4	5	6	7	8	9	1	2	3
28	2	3	4	5	6	7	8	9	1	2	3	4
29	3	4	5	6	7	8	9	1	2	3	4	5
30	4		6	7	8	9	1	2	3	4	5	6
31	5		7		9		2	3		5		7

Table 7. Port of Call Gateway for 2008

Day	Jan	Feb	Mar	Apr	May	Jun	Jul	Aug	Sep	Oct	Nov	Dec
To find your personal Port of Call, go down to your Birth Day, then across to your Birth Month to find your Personal Port of Call for 2008.												
1	3	4	5	6	7	8	9	1	2	3	4	5
2	4	5	6	7	8	9	1	2	3	4	5	6
3	5	6	7	8	9	1	2	3	4	5	6	7
4	6	7	8	9	1	2	3	4	5	6	7	8
5	7	8	9	1	2	3	4	5	6	7	8	9
6	8	9	1	2	3	4	5	6	7	8	9	1
7	9	1	2	3	4	5	6	7	8	9	1	2
8	1	2	3	4	5	6	7	8	9	1	2	3
9	2	3	4	5	6	7	8	9	1	2	3	4
10	3	4	5	6	7	8	9	1	2	3	4	5
11	4	5	6	7	8	9	1	2	3	4	5	6
12	5	6	7	8	9	1	2	3	4	5	6	7
13	6	7	8	9	1	2	3	4	5	6	7	8
14	7	8	9	1	2	3	4	5	6	7	8	9
15	8	9	1	2	3	4	5	6	7	8	9	1
16	9	1	2	3	4	5	6	7	8	9	1	2
17	1	2	3	4	5	6	7	8	9	1	2	3
18	2	3	4	5	6	7	8	9	1	2	3	4
19	3	4	5	6	7	8	9	1	2	3	4	5
20	4	5	6	7	8	9	1	2	3	4	5	6
21	5	6	7	8	9	1	2	3	4	5	6	7
22	6	7	8	9	1	2	3	4	5	6	7	8
23	7	8	9	1	2	3	4	5	6	7	8	9
24	8	9	1	2	3	4	5	6	7	8	9	1
25	9	1	2	3	4	5	6	7	8	9	1	2
26	1	2	3	4	5	6	7	8	9	1	2	3
27	2	3	4	5	6	7	8	9	1	2	3	4
28	3	4	5	6	7	8	9	1	2	3	4	5
29	4	5	6	7	8	9	1	2	3	4	5	6
30	5		7	8	9	1	2	3	4	5	6	7
31	6		8		1	2		4		6		8

Table 8. Port of Call Gateway for 2009

To find your personal Port of Call, go down to your Birth Day, then across to your Birth Month to find your Personal Port of Call for 2009.											
Day	Jan	Feb	Mar	Apr	May	Jun	Jul	Aug	Sep	Oct	Nov	Dec
1	4	5	6	7	8	9	1	2	3	4	5	6
2	5	6	7	8	9	1	2	3	4	5	6	7
3	6	7	8	9	1	2	3	4	5	6	7	8
4	7	8	9	1	2	3	4	5	6	7	8	9
5	8	9	1	2	3	4	5	6	7	8	9	1
6	9	1	2	3	4	5	6	7	8	9	1	2
7	1	2	3	4	5	6	7	8	9	1	2	3
8	2	3	4	5	6	7	8	9	1	2	3	4
9	3	4	5	6	7	8	9	1	2	3	4	5
10	4	5	6	7	8	9	1	2	3	4	5	6
11	5	6	7	8	9	1	2	3	4	5	6	7
12	6	7	8	9	1	2	3	4	5	6	7	8
13	7	8	9	1	2	3	4	5	6	7	8	9
14	8	9	1	2	3	4	5	6	7	8	9	1
15	9	1	2	3	4	5	6	7	8	9	1	2
16	1	2	3	4	5	6	7	8	9	1	2	3
17	2	3	4	5	6	7	8	9	1	2	3	4
18	3	4	5	6	7	8	9	1	2	3	4	5
19	4	5	6	7	8	9	1	2	3	4	5	6
20	5	6	7	8	9	1	2	3	4	5	6	7
21	6	7	8	9	1	2	3	4	5	6	7	8
22	7	8	9	1	2	3	4	5	6	7	8	9
23	8	9	1	2	3	4	5	6	7	8	9	1
24	9	1	2	3	4	5	6	7	8	9	1	2
25	1	2	3	4	5	6	7	8	9	1	2	3
26	2	3	4	5	6	7	8	9	1	2	3	4
27	3	4	5	6	7	8	9	1	2	3	4	5
28	4	5	6	7	8	9	1	2	3	4	5	6
29	5	6	7	8	9	1	2	3	4	5	6	7
30	6		8	9	1	2	3	4	5	6	7	8
31	7		9		2		4	5		7		9

Table 9. Port of Call Gateway for 2010

Day	Jan	Feb	Mar	Apr	May	Jun	Jul	Aug	Sep	Oct	Nov	Dec
To find your personal Port of Call, go down to your Birth Day, then across to your Birth Month to find your Personal Port of Call for 2010.												
1	5	6	7	8	9	1	2	3	4	5	6	7
2	6	7	8	9	1	2	3	4	5	6	7	8
3	7	8	9	1	2	3	4	5	6	7	8	9
4	8	9	1	2	3	4	5	6	7	8	9	1
5	9	1	2	3	4	5	6	7	8	9	1	2
6	1	2	3	4	5	6	7	8	9	1	2	3
7	2	3	4	5	6	7	8	9	1	2	3	4
8	3	4	5	6	7	8	9	1	2	3	4	5
9	4	5	6	7	8	9	1	2	3	4	5	6
10	5	6	7	8	9	1	2	3	4	5	6	7
11	6	7	8	9	1	2	3	4	5	6	7	8
12	7	8	9	1	2	3	4	5	6	7	8	9
13	8	9	1	2	3	4	5	6	7	8	9	1
14	9	1	2	3	4	5	6	7	8	9	1	2
15	1	2	3	4	5	6	7	8	9	1	2	3
16	2	3	4	5	6	7	8	9	1	2	3	4
17	3	4	5	6	7	8	9	1	2	3	4	5
18	4	5	6	7	8	9	1	2	3	4	5	6
19	5	6	7	8	9	1	2	3	4	5	6	7
20	6	7	8	9	1	2	3	4	5	6	7	8
21	7	8	9	1	2	3	4	5	6	7	8	9
22	8	9	1	2	3	4	5	6	7	8	9	1
23	9	1	2	3	4	5	6	7	8	9	1	2
24	1	2	3	4	5	6	7	8	9	1	2	3
25	2	3	4	5	6	7	8	9	1	2	3	4
26	3	4	5	6	7	8	9	1	2	3	4	5
27	4	5	6	7	8	9	1	2	3	4	5	6
28	5	6	7	8	9	1	2	3	4	5	6	7
29	6	7	8	9	1	2	3	4	5	6	7	8
30	7		9	1	2	3	4	5	6	7	8	9
31	8		1		3		5	6		8		1

Table 10. Port of Call Gateway for 2011

To find your personal Port of Call, go down to your Birth Day, then across to your Birth Month to find your Personal Port of Call for 2011.											
Day	Jan	Feb	Mar	Apr	May	Jun	Jul	Aug	Sep	Oct	Nov	Dec
1	6	7	8	9	1	2	3	4	5	6	7	8
2	7	8	9	1	2	3	4	5	6	7	8	9
3	8	9	1	2	3	4	5	6	7	8	9	1
4	9	1	2	3	4	5	6	7	8	9	1	2
5	1	2	3	4	5	6	7	8	9	1	2	3
6	2	3	4	5	6	7	8	9	1	2	3	4
7	3	4	5	6	7	8	9	1	2	3	4	5
8	4	5	6	7	8	9	1	2	3	4	5	6
9	5	6	7	8	9	1	2	3	4	5	6	7
10	6	7	8	9	1	2	3	4	5	6	7	8
11	7	8	9	1	2	3	4	5	6	7	8	9
12	8	9	1	2	3	4	5	6	7	8	9	1
13	9	1	2	3	4	5	6	7	8	9	1	2
14	1	2	3	4	5	6	7	8	9	1	2	3
15	2	3	4	5	6	7	8	9	1	2	3	4
16	3	4	5	6	7	8	9	1	2	3	4	5
17	4	5	6	7	8	9	1	2	3	4	5	6
18	5	6	7	8	9	1	2	3	4	5	6	7
19	6	7	8	9	1	2	3	4	5	6	7	8
20	7	8	9	1	2	3	4	5	6	7	8	9
21	8	9	1	2	3	4	5	6	7	8	9	1
22	9	1	2	3	4	5	6	7	8	9	1	2
23	1	2	3	4	5	6	7	8	9	1	2	3
24	2	3	4	5	6	7	8	9	1	2	3	4
25	3	4	5	6	7	8	9	1	2	3	4	5
26	4	5	6	7	8	9	1	2	3	4	5	6
27	5	6	7	8	9	1	2	3	4	5	6	7
28	6	7	8	9	1	2	3	4	5	6	7	8
29	7	8	9	1	2	3	4	5	6	7	8	9
30	8		1	2	3	4	5	6	7	8	9	1
31	9		2		4		6	7		9		2

Table 11. Port of Call Gateway for 2012

Day	Jan	Feb	Mar	Apr	May	Jun	Jul	Aug	Sep	Oct	Nov	Dec
To find your personal Port of Call, go down to your Birth Day, then across to your Birth Month to find your Personal Port of Call for 2012.											
1	7	8	9	1	2	3	4	5	6	7	8	9
2	8	9	1	2	3	4	5	6	7	8	9	1
3	9	1	2	3	4	5	6	7	8	9	1	2
4	1	2	3	4	5	6	7	8	9	1	2	3
5	2	3	4	5	6	7	8	9	1	2	3	4
6	3	4	5	6	7	8	9	1	2	3	4	5
7	4	5	6	7	8	9	1	2	3	4	5	6
8	5	6	7	8	9	1	2	3	4	5	6	7
9	6	7	8	9	1	2	3	4	5	6	7	8
10	7	8	9	1	2	3	4	5	6	7	8	9
11	8	9	1	2	3	4	5	6	7	8	9	1
12	9	1	2	3	4	5	6	7	8	9	1	2
13	1	2	3	4	5	6	7	8	9	1	2	3
14	2	3	4	5	6	7	8	9	1	2	3	4
15	3	4	5	6	7	8	9	1	2	3	4	5
16	4	5	6	7	8	9	1	2	3	4	5	6
17	5	6	7	8	9	1	2	3	4	5	6	7
18	6	7	8	9	1	2	3	4	5	6	7	8
19	7	8	9	1	2	3	4	5	6	7	8	9
20	8	9	1	2	3	4	5	6	7	8	9	1
21	9	1	2	3	4	5	6	7	8	9	1	2
22	1	2	3	4	5	6	7	8	9	1	2	3
23	2	3	4	5	6	7	8	9	1	2	3	4
24	3	4	5	6	7	8	9	1	2	3	4	5
25	4	5	6	7	8	9	1	2	3	4	5	6
26	5	6	7	8	9	1	2	3	4	5	6	7
27	6	7	8	9	1	2	3	4	5	6	7	8
28	7	8	9	1	2	3	4	5	6	7	8	9
29	8	9	1	2	3	4	5	6	7	8	9	1
30	9		2	3	4	5	6	7	8	9	1	2
31	1		3		5		7	8		1		3

Port of Call # 1

You have set sail on a new nine-year cycle in your life. Your passage will take you through nine gateways to change. Each Port of Call you reach holds a promise of fulfillment at the end of each 12-month journey.

Gateway to Independence

Never have you been more in control of the direction you navigate. You are at the helm. Between January 1ˢᵗ and December 31ˢᵗ, you are in command as you charter to your #1 Port of Call.

The tide is in. Now it is up to you to take the initiative to direct your course. New opportunities await you in all areas of your life. This is a very active year!

Business

Doors unlock presenting new career opportunities, especially during July. Accept a new job, be proud of a new promotion. Promote new contacts and accept recognition for your efforts.

Look forward to clear skies and open seas. October will be the point of no return. Your course is set. When you dock in December, reminisce over all the challenges you met during this year. You will be proud that you took an independent stand to launch new explorations. Expect to work on new goals as the year closes.

Personal

Men will be the prominent influence in your everyday affairs. This holds true whether you are male or female. If involved in a new relationship, you may find an intimate rendezvous delayed because business is focused before pleasure this year.

Travel / Locations

Chances are you may meet or transact business with people, who like yourself, are traveling in the #1 Port of Call year. If you are planning to relocate your business or residence, this is the year to go for it. Long distance moves are favored. You can start your life anew in April, May, August and September.

Log Notes

Everything in the universe operates in predictable, progressive cycles measured by the single digits 1 though 9. These numbers cover the entire spectrum of human experience.

Ancient mariners navigated the great deep by the sun, the moon and the stars. These luminaries dominate the sky and the rhythms of nature. They were reliable timepieces.

If the flood was the lucky time to be born, the ebb was the proper time to die, according to English lore. Sir John Falstaff died "at the turning o' the tide," and this was widely believed to be the moment when those with chronic or acute disease expired.

Samuel Eliot Morison wrote: "Just as farmers regulated plowing and sowing by the phases of the moon, so sailors and fishermen believed that the flood tide meant strength and the ebb tide meant weakness. If an old salt lay at death's door, his family and friends watched the tide. If he survived an ebb, he would improve with the flood, but he would always die on the ebb."

Port of Call # 2

You have set sail through another gateway to change. You are headed toward your #2 Port of Call in the present nine-year cycle of your life. Each Port of Call holds a promise of fulfillment at the end of each 12-month journey. As you travel the vibrational current of the number two, you will tune into your intuition.

Gateway to Cooperation

Between January 1st and December 31st, sunny skies may be shaded with cloudy thoughts. Fight fears of doubt with facts. Patience, tact and diplomacy are the buoys that float on the surface to guide you all year. Be prepared for some setbacks and delays in the Spring and Fall. You will find the atmosphere just opposite of last year.

Business

Financial winds blow steady, but the year may still be slow moving. Use caution with commercial ventures, unless they are directly related to last year's business projects.

Group activities and associations with large organizations are favored. All is not visible this year. Check all the fine details and be prepared for postponements. As winds subside, you may be required to submerge and cast your support to peers, coworkers or shipmates. Beware of undercurrents that can distract you and pull you off course.

Personal

Women's issues come to the fore this year. Expect dealings with mothers, grandmothers, sisters and aunts in the Spring and Fall. Very sensitive issues must be handled with discretion.

If single, your "dream-boat" or "dream-girl" may appear on the horizon. Keep a lookout in January, March and April. If you miss that connection, look again in late October and through the holidays.

Travel / Locations

Don't allow petty annoyances to become major rifts that can zap your emotional and physical energy. Plan times for rest and relaxation. A friendly wind suddenly springs up to blow your sails in May. You may find yourself steered to an out-of-the-way inlet where you can anchor and recuperate. You may find it desirable to share your experiences, so invite a travel companion. Trips by or across water beckon you. Take advantage of travel opportunities during the months of March, April, July, August and December. Chances are, you may meet or do business with people traveling in their #2 Port of Call year.

Log Notes

- *Divers in ancient times carried oil in their mouths to release beneath the surface when rough waters made their work difficult. Oil has a calming effect on the free waves of the open sea. You may be called upon to pour oil on troubled waters this year. Your counseling and mediation skills will be tested.*
- *Number two represents balance between two opposing points. For example: the right brain intuition (the Ying) and the left brain intellect (the Yang) are seeking harmony of expression.*

Port of Call # 3

You have set sail through another gateway to change. You are headed toward your #3 Port of Call in the present nine-year cycle of your life. Each year holds a promise of fulfillment at the end of each 12-month journey. The purpose is to help you grow and expand your horizons creatively and to flow freely.

Gateway to Self-Expression

Express the desires in your heart and let the child in you come out to play. Dare to dream like the child who envisions pictures and shapes in billowy clouds overhead. Between January 1st and December 31st, you will be surprised that many of your dreams can come true this year. Now is the time to advertise and to promote yourself. Any form of creative arts or ideas will be successful. It is an excellent year for communications through the channels of music, art, writing, lecturing and/or publications.

Business

Your fleet of merchant ships picks up a trade wind that brings luck to your commercial ventures. This is a good year for any type of sales work and a good year for investments. But try to avoid any change in employment. You will network to discuss a business venture, Ideas tossed around by agitated waters could prove to be a blessing in disguise. The outcome could well be an improved marketing concept. Brainstorm with positive thinkers.

Personal

Be prepared for personal emotions caught in the undertow of the devil's churn. There will be powerful temptations to enter into a clandestine love affair. Tread warily, as you may find it difficult for you to express your inner feelings. Unkind words can backlash causing you much regret or embarrassment.

Negative emotions scatter your energy and cause you to drift without purpose. Examine your personal relationships with telescopic focus and sort out your true feelings. Love affairs aside, your social life will escalate, especially revolving around creative aspects. Expect an abundance of communications and correspondence with friends and relatives. Know that negative news is destiny and out of your control. You can only control your reaction to it.

Travel / Locations

Many short trips are on the horizon. Enjoy yourself with friends and relatives. Be open to serendipity. Travel months strongly indicated are February, June, July and November. Chances are you may meet or do business with people traveling through the #3 Port of Call year.

Log Notes

- *The number three is symbolized by the triangle, which represents past, present, and future. It has long been a religious symbol of the trinity.*
- *The triangle also represents the three parts of the self: body, mind and soul.*
- *Number three represents artistic expression and communications. The creative life force is alive in you now.*
- *Music is an ageless expression of human feelings. For centuries, work songs of the sea, known as "shanties", have buoyed sailor's spirits throughout their adventures and their misfortunes over the seven seas.*

Port of Call # 4

You have set sail through another gateway to change. You are headed toward your #4 Port of Call in the present nine-year cycle of your life. Each year holds a promise of fulfillment at the end of each 12-month journey. Hold the wheel steady.

Gateway to Security

Anchor yourself and prepare for a year of extensive hours of both mental and physical work. Develop craftsmanship through self-discipline. You may feel that calm, dreary days are spent sitting and going nowhere. But this is the time to take inventory, check the manifests and scrape the barnacles. Make sure your vessel is watertight.

There are countless waypoints and routes to your destination. Continue plotting and mapping your course to your #4 Port of Call. You must decipher the light shifting breezes just as skillfully as you navigate the gusty winds of the high seas. This demands concentration to detail.

Sometimes when the restrictions seem unbearable, the only way to rise above is to use mental visualization. Tap into your spiritual faith and know that tremendous energy can be generated when the waters are held back, just as the ships passing through the Panama Canal must wait for the water to rise before the locks can be opened to allow forward sail again.

Business

Organize your work habits and stick to schedules. Financial responsibilities may feel like burdens, so be sure to stick to a budget. Although gambling and speculation are waypoints to disaster, this is an excellent year to sell property, settle lawsuits and market last year's products.

Personal

New friendships formed this year will last throughout your lifetime. Love and romance are difficult to keep afloat, but the end of the year will often bring a new relationship that will lead to something permanent. There are many reefs and barriers to romance. Those who maneuver through the obstacles and marry in a four vibration will find it will usually last.

Travel / Locations

Unless it is business related, you may decide against a change of residence or taking an extended trip this year. You may look for a quiet retreat in March in order to recharge your physical energy and buoy your spiritual and emotional health. Travel indicators are strongest for January, May, June and October. Chances are you may meet or do business with people traveling the #4 Port of Call year.

Log Notes

- *Universal meanings for the #4 are the elements (earth, air, fire and water), the four seasons, the four points of a compass and the four winds.*
- *The winds govern the moods and whim of the ocean. They frequently blow tempestuous, always restless and occasionally calm. The steadiest winds are the trades, blowing diagonally toward the Equator from the Northeast and Southwest.*

One ship drives east and one ship drives west
With the self-same winds that blow.
Tis the set of the sail and not the gales
Which tell us which way to go...

Ella Wheeler Wilcox, Winds of Fate

Port of Call # 5

You have set sail toward your #5 Port of Call in the present nine-year cycle of your life. Each year holds a promise of fulfillment at the end of each 12-month journey. One of the laws of physics is that the only constant is change. That is the law of five, the law of life.

Gateway to Adventure

Between January 1st and December 31st, you will experience many changes. Entrust yourself to the stars and signposts of the sea. Go for the gusto and take a chance. Lady Luck is at the helm to help you navigate challenge with the spirit of adventure.

Like the roving life of a sailor, this is the year to flow with changing conditions. Transition from smooth water to a broken sea is so sudden that no time is given for making arrangements.

Prepare to batten down, as it is difficult to see what may be going on in the distance. You will weather the fury that may be ahead to find the promised rainbow at the end of the storm.

Business

Opportunities come quickly and prolonged speculation will be the slippery fish that slides through your hands.

Finances fluctuate. There will be a strong tendency for reversals, good-to-bad, bad-to-good. The year is a whirlpool of activity, so reach for the handrails when seas get choppy. Life events will be as unpredictable as the sea.

Your best sailing is through the channels of communications. It is an excellent year for writing, speaking, performing creative arts, and advertising and sales work. Catch the crest of the wave for a good quick buy or sell.

Personal

Wherever your cruise takes you this year, you will feel the allure that will change the course of your destiny. Exotic ports entice you with five-star entertainment. Romance appears in all settings. Choose a setting of comfortable elegance or go for the glitz. You may encounter a handsome swashbuckler or a high-spirited sea-maiden to light up a sparkle on your ship after dark. Whether you share breakfast in bed or toast to champagne under the stars, diversity is matched only by the different ways to enjoy it all.

Travel / Locations

The key to smooth sailing is to use freedom constructively. It is a year of symphony to the senses: see, hear, touch, taste and smell. But try to avoid overindulgence in food, alcohol and sensual activity. Do not burn your bridges behind you. Hectic happenings and unexpected distractions carry strong tendency towards accidents, so do exercise caution in all things. Social activity flourishes and travel vibrations are strong during April, May and September. Keep a suitcase packed and ready for spur of the moment jaunts. Chances are you may meet or do business with people traveling the #5 Port of Call year.

Log Notes

- *"Chance is always powerful. Let your hook always be cast; in the pool where you least expect it, there will be a fish."* OVID
- *"Twenty years from now, you will be more disappointed by the things you didn't do, than by the ones that you did. So throw off the bowlines. Sail away from safe harbor. Catch the trade winds in your sails. Explore, Dream..."* Mark Twain

---

Port of Call # 6

You have set sail through another gateway to change. You are headed toward your #6 Port of Call in the present nine-year cycle of your life. Each year holds a promise of fulfillment at the end of each 12-month journey. Six represents the power of love, and control of the magical creative forces in nature that evolve from the equal union of the female and male energies.

Gateway to Family Harmony

Between January 1st and December 31st, you will find yourself cruising under sail with family and friends towards your #6 Port of Call. Service to home and community come into clear focus this year. You will not be able to sail around it. You must provide a nurturing environment. You will find yourself gathered round the galley to serve in the capacity as ship's cook, ship's counselor, ship's physician, the mother, father and lover. You will deal with a gamut of emotions expressing your loving concern to resolve issues and restore harmony. The demands made upon you by others will test your stamina.

You may not be prepared or willing to meet the duty and responsibilities to what is right or wrong, which may lead to quarrels or separations. Honesty, a sense of justice and fair play is important all year long. By sharing sincere concern, mutual respect and sensitivity to one another, you will challenge each other to excel in individual and shared responsibilities.

Business

This year may be slow moving financially, but the year is usually free of financial problems. The employment outcome will be good. Business partnerships formed under the influence of the number six should prove profitable. This year houses and property require a great deal of attention.

Expect to apply your artistic skills to remodel your present home should you choose not to buy a new one.

Personal

Home, in the heart of a sailor away at sea, may be envisioned as a cottage hidden in the trees in a small and private cove, or a mountainside with covered views of faraway places. Everyone pursues happiness, home, family and marriage. For those who are single, you will find this is a major marriage cycle. This wonderful year brings weddings, romance, reunions and celebrations influenced by traditional standards.

Heartwarming old-fashioned holiday vacations are a festive opportunity to get acquainted with new lovers, leading to marriage later in the year. Those who are already married will share the joy of newborns and christenings. The #6 Port of Call encompasses birth, death, marriage and divorce. The entire year is a family affair.

Travel / Locations

Book passage for a pleasure excursion on a holiday cruise liner or a luxurious riverboat sternwheeler. Find time to relax. Scan the scenery along the riverbank, read the mile post markers along the river or join an old-fashioned sing-a-long. River waters are a source of enlightenment in their own right. You will delight in another enriching waterway to self-discovery. Look for opportunities to travel in March, April, August and December. Chances are you may meet or do business with people traveling the #6 Port of Call year.

Log Notes

- FATHOM: *depth measurement of 6 feet.*
- REGATTAS: *events to attract young sailors in the spirit of competition, allowing them to test and refine their skills*

Port of Call # 7

You have set sail through another gateway to change in the present nine-year cycle of your life. You are headed toward your #7 Port of Call. Each year holds a promise of fulfillment at the end of each 12-month journey. Seven is associated with the moon and therefore is a number of reflections, symbolically reflected sunlight from the Moon.

Gateway to Wisdom

The mystical spirit of man is boundless as the sea. As a mystic explorer you have sailed on surface waves through gateways to seven Ports of Call. But be prepared to plummet the depths of your innermost being this year. Is there anyone on the bridge of self or are you just a vessel drifting on the tide of circumstance?

Between January 1st and December 31st, you will discover some profound spiritual insights about yourself, the universe and your place in it. After time spent at sea, exposed to the ravaging windswept waves, you will gratefully accept the #7 Port as a gift of security and repose. You will find yourself analyzing the momentous events of your own life and recall the feeling of life as you lived it. Eventually, the information resulting from your personal survey will direct your way. Like the evening star, the lighthouse points out the way for those who travel in darkness. You will find your own beacon of light glowing within.

Business

Commercial ambitions will not rule in now. It is time to perfect and analyze what is already in your life. You will attract money and recognition by following your natural instincts. In April, you may be feeling anxious, nervous or pressured. By June, you will feel your patience is being mercilessly tested. Because stress is often a barrier to self-fulfillment, you may lose your bearings and yearn for a solid resting point.

It may be well into October before you begin to sense new business goals. Your direction may surprise even you. You will navigate narrow passageways where big ships cannot go. The issue uppermost in your mind this year will be to know who and/or what is most critical to your achievements, personal success and happiness.

Personal

Romance and rendezvous are synonymous this year. The allure of mystery and intrigue will come unexpectedly to leave many haunting memories.

Travel / Locations

Coworkers and shipmates may misunderstand your moodiness and need for retreat. Reassure them that you only need time to regain your bearings. There is a mental bridge to cross. The subtle force of the number seven is operating to help you understand yourself. Trips to the sea or near the water and quiet country-sides will soothe and refresh your mind, body and spirit in February, July, September, November and December. Chances are you may meet or do business with people traveling the #7 Port of Call year.

Log Notes

Number seven symbolizes mystery, with study and knowledge as ways to explore the unknown and unseen.

- *7 governing planets used by the ancients*
- *7 days of the week*
- *7 notes on the musical scale*
- *7 wonders of the world*
- *7 deadly sins*
- *7 orders of architecture*
- *7 seas*

Port of Call # 8

You have set sail through another gateway to change in the present nine-year cycle of your life. You are headed toward your #8 Port of Call. Each year holds a promise of fulfillment at the end of each 12-month journey. Eight is part of the material world with the human body, the environment, money, possessions, status and achievement as a primary focus.

Gateway to Power and Financial Success

All the treasure map pieces now fit together to mark this as a year full of financial success and spiritual riches. Ride the waves that carry you to prosperity. Between January 1st and December 31st, a cornucopia of treasure comes spilling your way. Commercial endeavors of all kinds crest in the Fall to bring monetary payoffs from prior investments. Look for substantial benefits in all areas of your life.

Business

This is the ultimate year of action and accomplishment. Approach all opportunities in a businesslike manner. You will feel the power associated with the eight energy as job promotions and career status is highlighted. You can pick up an old or neglected enterprise and turn it to advantage and profit. Recognition will be forthcoming from shipmates and crew for the successful culmination of a special financial venture. Your organized competence and leadership will improve your professional standing and reputation.

Personal

Windfalls blow in from unexpected directions. A legacy or funds from government sources must be handled with efficiency and good judgment. Remember that an inheritance does not necessarily have to be associated

31

with a death. June and July bring changes in domestic matters. This is an excellent year to buy or sell real estate. Women, especially, can marry financially well under the influence of the eight in the quest for wealth and power.

Travel/ Locations

Travelers have gone about the globe as adventurers, conquerors, sightseers, nomads, scientists, migrants and merchants. Most travel will be business related in some manner. January, February, and June combine business and pleasure, while August will bring travel across water. October and November may bring overland travel in connection with property or the settling of a legacy. Chances are you may meet or do business with people traveling the #8 Port of Call year.

Log Notes

- *The oceans, which cover the major portions of the earth's surface, contain salt. Salt is an essential part of the human diet. Wherever salt is scarce, its value is very high. The word "salary" comes from the Latin salarium or salt money. Roman soldiers were often paid in salt, a necessary commodity in a hot climate.*
- *Piece of Eight: the Spanish dollar, or peso. It was marked with the figure 8.*
- *1670—The Spaniards paid for what things they bought in good Pillar pieces of Eight.*
- *1882—Peso was the monetary Unit of Central America, afterwards known as the Piece of Eight, and is the Mexican dollar of the present day.*

Port of Call # 9

You have set sail through another gateway to change in the present nine-year cycle of your life. Recap collected events from the preceding eight cycles of living as you sail toward your #9 Port of Call. Let experience be your guide to light the way for others as you set your sails for the next round of events.

Gateway to Universal Love

With each successive nine-year cycle, your knowledge is increased with your own life experience. You have touched many lives, just as they have touched your heart and soul. You are now a seasoned traveler. You have had your share of bad weather and sleepless nights, but there will also be sunlit days and picnics on the beach. You will embark again to discover another safe harbor and anchor at sundown at the end of your journey.

Between January 1st and December 31st, your greatest rewards come from giving to your fellow man. Satisfaction comes from giving without expectations of reward. Love and friendship are sometimes returned, often not. Many obligations are not repaid. This is the time to be charitable, generous and forgiving. Humanitarian pursuits bring their own personal rewards.

Business

Finances come in waves during the year. Money has a tendency to come in lump sums and dissipate in the same way. Expect substantial amounts of money from sales. Do not start a new business venture while the tide is out this year. Since this is a cycle of completion, any new ventures are pre-destined to failure. Do not sign any contracts or leases.

Personal

A bounty of romantic interludes will keep you off balance this year. New relationships will stir intense emotions. You will become entangled in an undertow of deep hidden currents. Most new romances will end by September. Enjoy the moment, but avoid marriage, unless the relationship was launched before January of the current year.

The number nine strikes a high water mark for separations and divorces this year. Existing relationships can run into trouble under rainy skies and gales. Problems carried over from three years ago must now be confronted with open and honest communications. This year also brings the end of business partnerships and even family ties. These conclusions may be bitter or sweet. They have fulfilled their spiritual purpose in your life. Some departures will be out of your control and you must learn to bend to the storms of "Mother Nature" and relinquish the helm with trust to the "Hands of God".

Travel/ Locations

Foreign shores will beckon to book international travel. You will log voyages long in miles as well as long in time. An atmosphere of brotherhood to encourage experiences that enrich the quality of life will enhance business or pleasure trips. Share the unique wonders of nature and life with brotherly love. If you are not the one traveling this year, expect someone from afar to visit you. Expect to reunite with friends from the past. Chances are you may meet or do business with people traveling the #9 Port of Call year.

Log Notes

Your current nine-year voyage has been a superb epic of courage and seamanship. No matter what the upcoming years may bring, you will live your life with new perspective, influenced by the power of numbers, the wisdom of the ancients and spiritual treasures without end.

All In The Same Boat

We're in this together; we all share the same risks. The literal origin is in the perils faced to people at sea, particularly in small boats during ancient times. The figurative meaning, which dominates today, was in print by 1584 in Thomas Hudson's poem Judith:

> *"Have Ye pain? So likewise pain have we:*
> *For in one boat we both embarked be."*

Treasure Maps
1 through 9

Monthly Influences

How to Find your Monthly Treasure Map

Each monthly vibration provides pointers to fulfillment. It identifies the forces that shape each month by offering suggestions for smoother sailing as you navigate the human sea of life.

- Look on Table 12, the monthly treasure map grid, to find your present year Port of Call Number.

- Then line up the Port of Call number to the current calendar month to find your monthly treasure map.

Example: Port of Call #3   = 3
+   Month of July   = 7
           Read Treasure Map: 1

Table 12. Treasure Map Grid

The 9 Year Cycle for Monthly Treasure Maps									
Port of Call	1	2	3	4	5	6	7	8	9
January	2	3	4	5	6	7	8	9	1
February	3	4	5	6	7	8	9	1	2
March	4	5	6	7	8	9	1	2	3
April	5	6	7	8	9	1	2	3	4
May	6	7	8	9	1	2	3	4	5
June	7	8	9	1	2	3	4	5	6
July	8	9	1	2	3	4	5	6	7
August	9	1	2	3	4	5	6	7	8
September	1	2	3	4	5	6	7	8	9
October	2	3	4	5	6	7	8	9	1
November	3	4	5	6	7	8	9	1	2
December	4	5	6	7	8	9	1	2	3

Treasure Map # 1
Monthly Influence

The people and experiences you encounter this month afford insights related to leadership, self-reliance, creativity and decision making.

It is always the unseen that most deeply stirs the imagination. You will be impatient to take the initiative on a special project. You will find yourself anxious to put yourself at the helm. But this is a tricky month. You must watch out for misunderstandings caused by unusual breakdowns in communications.

It may be month's end before conditions clear to allow you to travel long and far. A wise captain knows when to hoist anchor. Your final decision will cast you into international waters to sail beyond the point of no return. In retrospect, you will find the important decisions made this month will make a major impact on your future endeavors and their eventual outcome.

Keywords to Safe Ports

ambitious	independent	organizer
assertive	individualistic	self-reliant
creative	leader	

Keywords to Hidden Dangers

High Tide	Low Tide
aggressive	passive
arrogant	reluctant
stubborn	submissive

Treasure Map # 2
Monthly Influence

The people and experiences you encounter this month will afford valuable insights related to patience and cooperation. You must find the balance between giving and receiving.

Interactions with friends and loved ones are in the wind. Give up the helm and share responsibilities.

Don't be surprised if some developments take longer than expected. You may definitely feel a lull during the last two weeks of the month. Delays and temporary stoppages may be frustrating. You may sense a feeling of helplessness. Developments will progress of their own accord.

Keywords to Safe Ports

adaptable	considerate	receptive
amiable	flexible	supportive
caution	helpful	tolerant

Keywords to Hidden Dangers

High Tide	Low tide
condescending	careless
devious	inconsiderate
interfering	vacillating

Treasure Map # 3
Monthly Influence

The people and experiences you encounter this month will afford valuable insights into the sheer joy of living. Self-improvement and self-expression influence your activities all month long. Social contacts open channels to creativity and inspiration. All forms of communication are important now.

Don't allow gossip to turn negative. Harsh words can become heartbreakers. Words uttered in jealousy could backlash to cause unnecessary regrets.

Laughter is contagious. Enjoy yourself with friends by taking a short jaunt around the deck or go for a picnic on the beach. You will find joy in simple pleasures. Write a poem, paint a seascape. Visualize your goals!

Keywords to Safe Ports

communication	enthusiasm	optimism
creativity	expression	socialize
entertain	joie de vivre	travel

Keywords to Hidden Dangers

<u>High Tide</u>	<u>Low Tide</u>
Conceit	depression
exaggeration	jealousy
extravagance	spite

Treasure Map # 4
Monthly Influence

The people and experiences you encounter this month will afford valuable insights related to the need for order and discipline. There may be some economic limitations suggesting the need to budget finances. Contracts involving real estate come into focus. Consult with advisors associated with financial institutions and attorneys to promote and secure projects. Don't overlook details. Take a sharp view at the fine print.

This is a good month to schedule health care appointments. Don't procrastinate making that dental appointment. Mariners are practical people. They must be to survive. You, too, must be practical in all that you do this month. Accomplishment brings new responsibilities. You may have to adjust to a new work schedule. Don't allow yourself to become overwhelmed. Continue plotting and mapping the course to accomplish your goals. Your persistence will be rewarded.

Keywords to Safe Ports

concentration	endurance	perseverance
conservation	loyalty	preparation
discipline	moderation	reliability

Keywords to Hidden Dangers

High Tide	Low Tide
humorless	aimless
intolerance	inefficiency
narrow-mindedness	negligence

Treasure Map # 5
Monthly Influence

The people and experiences you encounter this month will afford valuable insights related to diversity. Look for a lively social agenda to fill your calendar this month. All kinds of wonderful things can happen. Expect a few surprises as you mingle with stimulating people. You will attract people from all walks of life. New opportunities will emerge through these contacts, providing an outlet to express your ideas.

Life steers us in new directions when we least expect it. Sailors thrive on challenge. Keep alert to financial and business opportunities and you will be able to make the right moves and decisions when the winds shift in your favor. Quick travel trips and lots of variety set the pace. Sail is about change in style, in attitudes, and how we live our lives. Be prepared to change course midstream. You can't change the wind, but you can adjust your sails. Stay flexible!

Keywords to Safe Ports

adventure	enthusiastic	spontaneous
change	flexible	unconventional
challenge	progressive	venturesome

Keywords to Hidden Dangers

High Tide	Low Tide
irresponsible	conforming
over-indulgent	narrow-minded
thoughtless	old-fashioned

Treasure Map # 6
Monthly Influence

The people and experiences you encounter this month will afford valuable insights related to responsibilities associated with home, family and loved ones. Issues arise that require you to sacrifice personal desires for a member of your inner circle. You must maintain personal integrity with all those who seek your assistance.

This month will be filled with news of engagements, weddings, christenings and celebrations. Don't be surprised to hear of some postponements or broken engagements that will touch you personally. Snags will pull you into a whirlpool of emotions, only to become a blessing in disguise by month's end. The lesson of harmony can be a meaningful one. A friend will be grateful to you for mediating a difficult situation.

Others will find artistic pursuits, such as music, painting, or home decorating an excellent outlet. Those traveling might find plans delayed. Keep medications accessible when traveling by air. There will be a strong possibility that luggage can be lost or misrouted.

Keywords to Safe Ports

compassion	devotion	nurturing
concern for family	generosity	peace-making
counseling	healing	teaching

Keywords to Hidden Dangers

High Tide	Low Tide
critical	opinionated
interfering	prejudiced
possessive	unforgiving

Treasure Map # 7
Monthly Influence

The people and experiences you encounter this month will afford valuable insights related to mental analysis and deep understanding. Situations arise to challenge your ability to accept reality. Clear passage is veiled in an atmosphere of secrecy. You may feel isolated and disconnected from the real world of everyday living. Foggy doubts seep within to induce anxiety surrounding business and material interests. Personal relationships feel distant. Communications are many times misunderstood, causing emotional rifts.

Full stop! Drop and set anchor. Center yourself by tuning into your inner faith. Immerse yourself into your inner being and learn the value of solitude. Success swells with the law of attraction this month. Take stock of long-term situations. Take the time to ponder your life goals and expect the best before weighing anchor. Contemplation of the mysteries of life brings profound spiritual insights. You will be blessed with the quiet rewards of wisdom that comes from fathoming your deepest intuitions.

Keywords to Safe Ports

analytical	inquisitive	poised
contemplative	introspective	refined
discriminating	mystical	wise

Keywords to Hidden Dangers

High Tide	Low Tide
antisocial	forgetful
fearful	naive
secretive	unenlightened

44

Treasure Map # 8
Monthly Influence

The people and experiences you encounter this month offer valuable insights related to the purpose of money and personal power.

Landlubbers, as well as shipmates and crew, will test your authority. You will be challenged to demonstrate your abilities to maintain the helm. Endurance and performance under pressure will be essential qualities to any winning effort. Your strength provides power to adjust sails to propel you forward and keep you on course. You will skipper a winning ship by focusing on eliminating friction using your organizational and managerial abilities.

Prosperity is in the air. Windfalls appear from unexpected sources. Opportunities abound and recognition can be on the horizon shaping into a promotion, an offered partnership, or an inheritance. Institutions and government sources will approve loans and/or grants.

Eight is an action month. It is an excellent cycle to deal with real estate. Legal issues should be resolved to your satisfaction.

Keywords to Safe Ports

assertive	diplomatic	organized
businesslike	discriminating	self-reliant
confident	efficient	strong

Keywords to Hidden Dangers

High Tide	Low Tide
abusive	disreputable
chauvinistic	indifferent
selfish	negligent

Treasure Map # 9
Monthly Influence

The people and experiences you encounter this month afford insights into cherishing the moment and learning to let go. This month will be filled with drama and emotions of high intensity. A situation involving work or a loved one may prove difficult. The completion of a project or the ending of a personal relationship will test your character. The completion may not be your decision. If not, know that life sometimes listens to a higher command. The ultimate outcome will prove beneficial over time.

This month will also bring insights into the valuable lesson of forgiveness. Personal crisis brings opportunities for self-discovery. Mistakes, big or small, come in guise like maritime vagrants, smugglers and pirates on the high seas to rob you of the joy in your life. Allow yourself to learn from trial and error and to learn from your mistakes. After all, you are only human. Learn to forgive yourself as well as to forgive others. It is a time to be kind and compassionate. Do not expect rewards when assisting others, whatever the situation.

With or without endings, you will find expression through artistic creation. You will be inspired to use your imagination in your art, music and writing.

Keywords to Safe Ports

artistic	humanitarian	philanthropic
charitable	intuitive	spiritual
courageous	liberal	trustworthy

Keywords to Hidden Dangers

High Tide	Low Tide
biased	insensitive
impractical	stubborn
self-centered	unforgiving

Daily Compass Points
1 through 9

Daily Influences

Find Your Daily Compass Point

Keep alert to the trend of thoughts and actions each day suggests. Make better informed decisions, exercising your free will and freedom of choice on a daily basis.

- Find your Personal Port of Call for the current year (see Tables 1 through 11).

- Look for the Compass Point for your Port of Call for the current year (see Tables 13 through 21).

- Find the current calendar month.

- Line the current calendar month up with the current calendar day.

- Then turn to the Daily Compass Points on the next page to read the synopsis for the Daily Compass Point for that day.

For Example:

If you are in a #3 Port of Call this year, you would see Compass Point for Port of Call #3 (Table 15) to find your daily compass point. For instance, if today's date were March 7th, you would read Daily Compass Point #4. See sample breakout of Table 15 below:

Compass Point Example for March 7
in Port of Call Year #3

Table 15. Compass Point #3					
Jan	Feb	**Mar**	Apr	May	Jun
Day	Daily Compass Point				
1	5	6	7	8	9	1
2	6	7	8	9	1	2
3	7	8	9	1	2	3
4	8	9	1	2	3	4
5	9	1	2	3	4	5
6	1	2	3	4	5	6
7	2	3	4	5	6	7
8	3	4	5	6	7	8

Daily Compass Points

Daily Compass Point #1
- Plan an action day with purpose.
- Cast off with confidence. Lack of initiative may result in floundering.
- Fresh focus and a determined attitude will open new channels to any situation you want to promote.

Daily Compass Point #2
- Focus your attention.
- Don't make waves or force confrontations. This is not a day to push for results.
- Take your time, gather facts, observe details and test the waters, while maintaining a calm exposure.

Daily Compass Point #3
- SMILE ! ☺ Be positive and optimistic.
- Loose lips sink ships, so watch your words. The urge to talk, talk, talk will be strong. Stifle talk about personal anxieties. Refuse to worry.
- Load the children and pets in the dinghy and take a vacation play day.

Daily Compass Point #4
- Work with perseverance, for tomorrow you must be flexible.
- Pay attention to details and square up mistakes by making necessary adjustments.
- Complete projects at hand.

Daily Compass Point #5
- Accept the unexpected and go with the flow.

- Be open to new opportunities and new contacts.
- Take a trip, for a change of scene.

Daily Compass Point #6

- Domestic feelings surface. Family matters arise. Expect home changes and children's issues to come to the forefront.
- Volunteer your assistance to help teach and counsel.
- Allow others to learn from your example to avoid dependency. Try not to meddle; offer advice only if asked.

Daily Compass Point #7

- Anchor yourself. This is a day to rest, meditate and reflect.
- Dive beneath surface values.
- Enjoy silence, peace and solitude in nature.

Daily Compass Point #8

- Action leads to success.
- Schedule business appointments, sign contracts, and address legal issues.
- Be an ambitious leader. Assert your executive ability in business endeavors. If you feel you do not fit in, then stand out. Be unique!
- Recognize yourself as an achiever while maintaining the balance between your material and spiritual nature.

Daily Compass Point #9

- Humanitarian interests highlight your day.
- Show compassion, empathy and forgiveness.
- Understand the difference between being charitable and acting out of pity.
- Finish projects today.
- Swab the decks—physically and mentally.

Table 13. Compass Point for Port of Call #1

Day	Jan	Feb	Mar	Apr	May	Jun	Jul	Aug	Sep	Oct	Nov	Dec
Go down to the current day, then go across to the current month to find your daily Compass Point.												
1	3	4	5	6	7	8	9	1	2	3	4	5
2	4	5	6	7	8	9	1	2	3	4	5	6
3	5	6	7	8	9	1	2	3	4	5	6	7
4	6	7	8	9	1	2	3	4	5	6	7	8
5	7	8	9	1	2	3	4	5	6	7	8	9
6	8	9	1	2	3	4	5	6	7	8	9	1
7	9	1	2	3	4	5	6	7	8	9	1	2
8	1	2	3	4	5	6	7	8	9	1	2	3
9	2	3	4	5	6	7	8	9	1	2	3	4
10	3	4	5	6	7	8	9	1	2	3	4	5
11	4	5	6	7	8	9	1	2	3	4	5	6
12	5	6	7	8	9	1	2	3	4	5	6	7
13	6	7	8	9	1	2	3	4	5	6	7	8
14	7	8	9	1	2	3	4	5	6	7	8	9
15	8	9	1	2	3	4	5	6	7	8	9	1
16	9	1	2	3	4	5	6	7	8	9	1	2
17	1	2	3	4	5	6	7	8	9	1	2	3
18	2	3	4	5	6	7	8	9	1	2	3	4
19	3	4	5	6	7	8	9	1	2	3	4	5
20	4	5	6	7	8	9	1	2	3	4	5	6
21	5	6	7	8	9	1	2	3	4	5	6	7
22	6	7	8	9	1	2	3	4	5	6	7	8
23	7	8	9	1	2	3	4	5	6	7	8	9
24	8	9	1	2	3	4	5	6	7	8	9	1
25	9	1	2	3	4	5	6	7	8	9	1	2
26	1	2	3	4	5	6	7	8	9	1	2	3
27	2	3	4	5	6	7	8	9	1	2	3	4
28	3	4	5	6	7	8	9	1	2	3	4	5
29	4	5	6	7	8	9	1	2	3	4	5	6
30	5		7	8	9	1	2	3	4	5	6	7
31	6		8		1	2		4		6		8

Table 14. Compass Point for Port of Call #2

Day	Jan	Feb	Mar	Apr	May	Jun	Jul	Aug	Sep	Oct	Nov	Dec
Go down to the current day, then go across to the current month to find your daily Compass Point.												
1	4	5	6	7	8	9	1	2	3	4	5	6
2	5	6	7	8	9	1	2	3	4	5	6	7
3	6	7	8	9	1	2	3	4	5	6	7	8
4	7	8	9	1	2	3	4	5	6	7	8	9
5	8	9	1	2	3	4	5	6	7	8	9	1
6	9	1	2	3	4	5	6	7	8	9	1	2
7	1	2	3	4	5	6	7	8	9	1	2	3
8	2	3	4	5	6	7	8	9	1	2	3	4
9	3	4	5	6	7	8	9	1	2	3	4	5
10	4	5	6	7	8	9	1	2	3	4	5	6
11	5	6	7	8	9	1	2	3	4	5	6	7
12	6	7	8	9	1	2	3	4	5	6	7	8
13	7	8	9	1	2	3	4	5	6	7	8	9
14	8	9	1	2	3	4	5	6	7	8	9	1
15	9	1	2	3	4	5	6	7	8	9	1	2
16	1	2	3	4	5	6	7	8	9	1	2	3
17	2	3	4	5	6	7	8	9	1	2	3	4
18	3	4	5	6	7	8	9	1	2	3	4	5
19	4	5	6	7	8	9	1	2	3	4	5	6
20	5	6	7	8	9	1	2	3	4	5	6	7
21	6	7	8	9	1	2	3	4	5	6	7	8
22	7	8	9	1	2	3	4	5	6	7	8	9
23	8	9	1	2	3	4	5	6	7	8	9	1
24	9	1	2	3	4	5	6	7	8	9	1	2
25	1	2	3	4	5	6	7	8	9	1	2	3
26	2	3	4	5	6	7	8	9	1	2	3	4
27	3	4	5	6	7	8	9	1	2	3	4	5
28	4	5	6	7	8	9	1	2	3	4	5	6
29	5	6	7	8	9	1	2	3	4	5	6	7
30	6		8	9	1	2	3	4	5	6	7	8
31	7		9		2		4	5		7		9

Table 15. Compass Point for Port of Call #3

	Go down to the current day, then go across to the current month to find your daily Compass Point.										
Day	Jan	Feb	Mar	Apr	May	Jun	Jul	Aug	Sep	Oct	Nov	Dec
1	5	6	7	8	9	1	2	3	4	5	6	7
2	6	7	8	9	1	2	3	4	5	6	7	8
3	7	8	9	1	2	3	4	5	6	7	8	9
4	8	9	1	2	3	4	5	6	7	8	9	1
5	9	1	2	3	4	5	6	7	8	9	1	2
6	1	2	3	4	5	6	7	8	9	1	2	3
7	2	3	4	5	6	7	8	9	1	2	3	4
8	3	4	5	6	7	8	9	1	2	3	4	5
9	4	5	6	7	8	9	1	2	3	4	5	6
10	5	6	7	8	9	1	2	3	4	5	6	7
11	6	7	8	9	1	2	3	4	5	6	7	8
12	7	8	9	1	2	3	4	5	6	7	8	9
13	8	9	1	2	3	4	5	6	7	8	9	1
14	9	1	2	3	4	5	6	7	8	9	1	2
15	1	2	3	4	5	6	7	8	9	1	2	3
16	2	3	4	5	6	7	8	9	1	2	3	4
17	3	4	5	6	7	8	9	1	2	3	4	5
18	4	5	6	7	8	9	1	2	3	4	5	6
19	5	6	7	8	9	1	2	3	4	5	6	7
20	6	7	8	9	1	2	3	4	5	6	7	8
21	7	8	9	1	2	3	4	5	6	7	8	9
22	8	9	1	2	3	4	5	6	7	8	9	1
23	9	1	2	3	4	5	6	7	8	9	1	2
24	1	2	3	4	5	6	7	8	9	1	2	3
25	2	3	4	5	6	7	8	9	1	2	3	4
26	3	4	5	6	7	8	9	1	2	3	4	5
27	4	5	6	7	8	9	1	2	3	4	5	6
28	5	6	7	8	9	1	2	3	4	5	6	7
29	6	7	8	9	1	2	3	4	5	6	7	8
30	7		9	1	2	3	4	5	6	7	8	9
31	8		1		3		5	6		8		1

Table 16. Compass Point for Port of Call #4

Day	Go down to the current day, then go across to the current month to find your daily Compass Point.											
	Jan	Feb	Mar	Apr	May	Jun	Jul	Aug	Sep	Oct	Nov	Dec
1	6	7	8	9	1	2	3	4	5	6	7	8
2	7	8	9	1	2	3	4	5	6	7	8	9
3	8	9	1	2	3	4	5	6	7	8	9	1
4	9	1	2	3	4	5	6	7	8	9	1	2
5	1	2	3	4	5	6	7	8	9	1	2	3
6	2	3	4	5	6	7	8	9	1	2	3	4
7	3	4	5	6	7	8	9	1	2	3	4	5
8	4	5	6	7	8	9	1	2	3	4	5	6
9	5	6	7	8	9	1	2	3	4	5	6	7
10	6	7	8	9	1	2	3	4	5	6	7	8
11	7	8	9	1	2	3	4	5	6	7	8	9
12	8	9	1	2	3	4	5	6	7	8	9	1
13	9	1	2	3	4	5	6	7	8	9	1	2
14	1	2	3	4	5	6	7	8	9	1	2	3
15	2	3	4	5	6	7	8	9	1	2	3	4
16	3	4	5	6	7	8	9	1	2	3	4	5
17	4	5	6	7	8	9	1	2	3	4	5	6
18	5	6	7	8	9	1	2	3	4	5	6	7
19	6	7	8	9	1	2	3	4	5	6	7	8
20	7	8	9	1	2	3	4	5	6	7	8	9
21	8	9	1	2	3	4	5	6	7	8	9	1
22	9	1	2	3	4	5	6	7	8	9	1	2
23	1	2	3	4	5	6	7	8	9	1	2	3
24	2	3	4	5	6	7	8	9	1	2	3	4
25	3	4	5	6	7	8	9	1	2	3	4	5
26	4	5	6	7	8	9	1	2	3	4	5	6
27	5	6	7	8	9	1	2	3	4	5	6	7
28	6	7	8	9	1	2	3	4	5	6	7	8
29	7	8	9	1	2	3	4	5	6	7	8	9
30	8		1	2	3	4	5	6	7	8	9	1
31	9		2		4		6	7		9		2

Table 17. Compass Point for Port of Call #5

					Go down to the current day, then go across to the current month to find your daily Compass Point.							
Day	Jan	Feb	Mar	Apr	May	Jun	Jul	Aug	Sep	Oct	Nov	Dec
1	7	8	9	1	2	3	4	5	6	7	8	9
2	8	9	1	2	3	4	5	6	7	8	9	1
3	9	1	2	3	4	5	6	7	8	9	1	2
4	1	2	3	4	5	6	7	8	9	1	2	3
5	2	3	4	5	6	7	8	9	1	2	3	4
6	3	4	5	6	7	8	9	1	2	3	4	5
7	4	5	6	7	8	9	1	2	3	4	5	6
8	5	6	7	8	9	1	2	3	4	5	6	7
9	6	7	8	9	1	2	3	4	5	6	7	8
10	7	8	9	1	2	3	4	5	6	7	8	9
11	8	9	1	2	3	4	5	6	7	8	9	1
12	9	1	2	3	4	5	6	7	8	9	1	2
13	1	2	3	4	5	6	7	8	9	1	2	3
14	2	3	4	5	6	7	8	9	1	2	3	4
15	3	4	5	6	7	8	9	1	2	3	4	5
16	4	5	6	7	8	9	1	2	3	4	5	6
17	5	6	7	8	9	1	2	3	4	5	6	7
18	6	7	8	9	1	2	3	4	5	6	7	8
19	7	8	9	1	2	3	4	5	6	7	8	9
20	8	9	1	2	3	4	5	6	7	8	9	1
21	9	1	2	3	4	5	6	7	8	9	1	2
22	1	2	3	4	5	6	7	8	9	1	2	3
23	2	3	4	5	6	7	8	9	1	2	3	4
24	3	4	5	6	7	8	9	1	2	3	4	5
25	4	5	6	7	8	9	1	2	3	4	5	6
26	5	6	7	8	9	1	2	3	4	5	6	7
27	6	7	8	9	1	2	3	4	5	6	7	8
28	7	8	9	1	2	3	4	5	6	7	8	9
29	8	9	1	2	3	4	5	6	7	8	9	1
30	9		2	3	4	5	6	7	8	9	1	2
31	1		3		5		7	8		1		3

Table 18. Compass Point for Port of Call #6

	Go down to the current day, then go across to the current month to find your daily Compass Point.										
Day	Jan	Feb	Mar	Apr	May	Jun	Jul	Aug	Sep	Oct	Nov	Dec
1	8	9	1	2	3	4	5	6	7	8	9	1
2	9	1	2	3	4	5	6	7	8	9	1	2
3	1	2	3	4	5	6	7	8	9	1	2	3
4	2	3	4	5	6	7	8	9	1	2	3	4
5	3	4	5	6	7	8	9	1	2	3	4	5
6	4	5	6	7	8	9	1	2	3	4	5	6
7	5	6	7	8	9	1	2	3	4	5	6	7
8	6	7	8	9	1	2	3	4	5	6	7	8
9	7	8	9	1	2	3	4	5	6	7	8	9
10	8	9	1	2	3	4	5	6	7	8	9	1
11	9	1	2	3	4	5	6	7	8	9	1	2
12	1	2	3	4	5	6	7	8	9	1	2	3
13	2	3	4	5	6	7	8	9	1	2	3	4
14	3	4	5	6	7	8	9	1	2	3	4	5
15	4	5	6	7	8	9	1	2	3	4	5	6
16	5	6	7	8	9	1	2	3	4	5	6	7
17	6	7	8	9	1	2	3	4	5	6	7	8
18	7	8	9	1	2	3	4	5	6	7	8	9
19	8	9	1	2	3	4	5	6	7	8	9	1
20	9	1	2	3	4	5	6	7	8	9	1	2
21	1	2	3	4	5	6	7	8	9	1	2	3
22	2	3	4	5	6	7	8	9	1	2	3	4
23	3	4	5	6	7	8	9	1	2	3	4	5
24	4	5	6	7	8	9	1	2	3	4	5	6
25	5	6	7	8	9	1	2	3	4	5	6	7
26	6	7	8	9	1	2	3	4	5	6	7	8
27	7	8	9	1	2	3	4	5	6	7	8	9
28	8	9	1	2	3	4	5	6	7	8	9	1
29	9	1	2	3	4	5	6	7	8	9	1	2
30	1		3	4	5	6	7	8	9	1	2	3
31	2		4		6		8	9		2		4

Table 19. Compass Point for Port of Call #7

					Go down to the current day, then go across to the current month to find your daily Compass Point.						
Day	Jan	Feb	Mar	Apr	May	Jun	Jul	Aug	Sep	Oct	Nov	Dec
1	9	1	2	3	4	5	6	7	8	9	1	2
2	1	2	3	4	5	6	7	8	9	1	2	3
3	2	3	4	5	6	7	8	9	1	2	3	4
4	3	4	5	6	7	8	9	1	2	3	4	5
5	4	5	6	7	8	9	1	2	3	4	5	6
6	5	6	7	8	9	1	2	3	4	5	6	7
7	6	7	8	9	1	2	3	4	5	6	7	8
8	7	8	9	1	2	3	4	5	6	7	8	9
9	8	9	1	2	3	4	5	6	7	8	9	1
10	9	1	2	3	4	5	6	7	8	9	1	2
11	1	2	3	4	5	6	7	8	9	1	2	3
12	2	3	4	5	6	7	8	9	1	2	3	4
13	3	4	5	6	7	8	9	1	2	3	4	5
14	4	5	6	7	8	9	1	2	3	4	5	6
15	5	6	7	8	9	1	2	3	4	5	6	7
16	6	7	8	9	1	2	3	4	5	6	7	8
17	7	8	9	1	2	3	4	5	6	7	8	9
18	8	9	1	2	3	4	5	6	7	8	9	1
19	9	1	2	3	4	5	6	7	8	9	1	2
20	1	2	3	4	5	6	7	8	9	1	2	3
21	2	3	4	5	6	7	8	9	1	2	3	4
22	3	4	5	6	7	8	9	1	2	3	4	5
23	4	5	6	7	8	9	1	2	3	4	5	6
24	5	6	7	8	9	1	2	3	4	5	6	7
25	6	7	8	9	1	2	3	4	5	6	7	8
26	7	8	9	1	2	3	4	5	6	7	8	9
27	8	9	1	2	3	4	5	6	7	8	9	1
28	9	1	2	3	4	5	6	7	8	9	1	2
29	1	2	3	4	5	6	7	8	9	1	2	3
30	2		4	5	6	7	8	9	1	2	3	4
31	3		5		7		9	1		3		5

Table 20. Compass Point for Port of Call #8

Day	Jan	Feb	Mar	Apr	May	Jun	Jul	Aug	Sep	Oct	Nov	Dec
	Go down to the current day, then go across to the current month to find your daily Compass Point.										
1	1	2	3	4	5	6	7	8	9	1	2	3
2	2	3	4	5	6	7	8	9	1	2	3	4
3	3	4	5	6	7	8	9	1	2	3	4	5
4	4	5	6	7	8	9	1	2	3	4	5	6
5	5	6	7	8	9	1	2	3	4	5	6	7
6	6	7	8	9	1	2	3	4	5	6	7	8
7	7	8	9	1	2	3	4	5	6	7	8	9
8	8	9	1	2	3	4	5	6	7	8	9	1
9	9	1	2	3	4	5	6	7	8	9	1	2
10	1	2	3	4	5	6	7	8	9	1	2	3
11	2	3	4	5	6	7	8	9	1	2	3	4
12	3	4	5	6	7	8	9	1	2	3	4	5
13	4	5	6	7	8	9	1	2	3	4	5	6
14	5	6	7	8	9	1	2	3	4	5	6	7
15	6	7	8	9	1	2	3	4	5	6	7	8
16	7	8	9	1	2	3	4	5	6	7	8	9
17	8	9	1	2	3	4	5	6	7	8	9	1
18	9	1	2	3	4	5	6	7	8	9	1	2
19	1	2	3	4	5	6	7	8	9	1	2	3
20	2	3	4	5	6	7	8	9	1	2	3	4
21	3	4	5	6	7	8	9	1	2	3	4	5
22	4	5	6	7	8	9	1	2	3	4	5	6
23	5	6	7	8	9	1	2	3	4	5	6	7
24	6	7	8	9	1	2	3	4	5	6	7	8
25	7	8	9	1	2	3	4	5	6	7	8	9
26	8	9	1	2	3	4	5	6	7	8	9	1
27	9	1	2	3	4	5	6	7	8	9	1	2
28	1	2	3	4	5	6	7	8	9	1	2	3
29	2	3	4	5	6	7	8	9	1	2	3	4
30	3		5	6	7	8	9	1	2	3	4	5
31	4		6		8		1	2		4		6

Table 21. Compass Point for Port of Call #9

Day	Jan	Feb	Mar	Apr	May	Jun	Jul	Aug	Sep	Oct	Nov	Dec
	Go down to the current day, then go across to the current month to find your daily Compass Point.											
1	2	3	4	5	6	7	8	9	1	2	3	4
2	3	4	5	6	7	8	9	1	2	3	4	5
3	4	5	6	7	8	9	1	2	3	4	5	6
4	5	6	7	8	9	1	2	3	4	5	6	7
5	6	7	8	9	1	2	3	4	5	6	7	8
6	7	8	9	1	2	3	4	5	6	7	8	9
7	8	9	1	2	3	4	5	6	7	8	9	1
8	9	1	2	3	4	5	6	7	8	9	1	2
9	1	2	3	4	5	6	7	8	9	1	2	3
10	2	3	4	5	6	7	8	9	1	2	3	4
11	3	4	5	6	7	8	9	1	2	3	4	5
12	4	5	6	7	8	9	1	2	3	4	5	6
13	5	6	7	8	9	1	2	3	4	5	6	7
14	6	7	8	9	1	2	3	4	5	6	7	8
15	7	8	9	1	2	3	4	5	6	7	8	9
16	8	9	1	2	3	4	5	6	7	8	9	1
17	9	1	2	3	4	5	6	7	8	9	1	2
18	1	2	3	4	5	6	7	8	9	1	2	3
19	2	3	4	5	6	7	8	9	1	2	3	4
20	3	4	5	6	7	8	9	1	2	3	4	5
21	4	5	6	7	8	9	1	2	3	4	5	6
22	5	6	7	8	9	1	2	3	4	5	6	7
23	6	7	8	9	1	2	3	4	5	6	7	8
24	7	8	9	1	2	3	4	5	6	7	8	9
25	8	9	1	2	3	4	5	6	7	8	9	1
26	9	1	2	3	4	5	6	7	8	9	1	2
27	1	2	3	4	5	6	7	8	9	1	2	3
28	2	3	4	5	6	7	8	9	1	2	3	4
29	3	4	5	6	7	8	9	1	2	3	4	5
30	4		6	7	8	9	1	2	3	4	5	6
31	5		7		9		2	3		5		7

Anchor Points
1 through 9

Travel / Vacation

Where To Anchor

*Certain places have a profound affect on your health,
happiness, success and prosperity.*

Choosing a city to live in can be a puzzle, but your birth number is the key to unlock the mystery. You will always find opportunity for growth and development in a city having the same vibration as the day of your birth. You can be sure you will have more fun and fortune at places ruled by your number.

Astrology and numerology are both incorporated in Table 22 and are used to determine the best places for you to live or vacation. There are 9 numbers and each number has its planet. The planets exhibit certain characteristics and therefore each number has is own characteristics.

Table 22. Numeric Characteristics

No.	Planet	Basic Characteristics	Dates
1	Sun	Will, determination, dignity, confidence, reliance, vitality, loyalty, poise, fortitude, optimism	1st, 10th, 19th, 28th
2	Moon	Matter, will, feeling, maternal, flexibility, sensitivity, receptivity, imagination, domesticity, sympathy	2nd, 11th, 20th, 29th
3	Jupiter	Aspiration, generosity, benevolence, religion, expansion, optimism, humane, mercy, and dignity	3rd, 12th, 21st, 30th
4	Uranus	Independence, freedom, originality, genius, intuition, unconventional, unexpected, idealism, reformer, impersonal	4th, 13th, 22nd, 31st
5	Mercury	Reason, agility, duality, expressiveness, analytic, adaptable, changeable, communicative	5th, 14th, 23rd
6	Venus	Beauty, love, art, sociability, femininity, gentleness, Refinement, cooperative, originality	6th, 15th, 24th
7	Neptune	Sensitivity, inspiration, compassion, emotion, imagination, clairvoyance, universal love, sacrifice	7th, 16th, 25th
8	Saturn	Caution, restraint, sincerity, stability, justice, law, karma	8th, 17th, 26th
9	Mars	Energy, passion, leadership, impulsive, courage, forceful, independent, practical	9th, 18th, 27th
		Travel locations are presented by the best locations based on your day of birth followed by locations most harmonious	

Anchor Points

Born on the 1st, 10th, 19th or 28th

United States

- Connecticut, Idaho, Michigan, North Dakota, Rhode Island

Harmonious Locations:

- Alabama, Alaska, California, Colorado, Florida, Illinois, Indiana, Kansas, Kentucky, Louisiana, Maryland, Minnesota, Mississippi, Nevada, New Hampshire, New Jersey, North Carolina, Oklahoma, Oregon, South Dakota, Washington

Cities Worldwide

- Amsterdam, Caan, Cairo, Chicago, Detroit, Hong Kong, Los Angeles, Louisville, Milwaukee, Minneapolis, Portland, Sacramento, Sao Paulo, Scottsdale, Seattle, Simi Valley, Tulsa

Harmonious Locations:

- Amarillo, Amsterdam, Anchorage, Augusta, Bakersfield, Birmingham, Bombay, Bonn, Boston, Buenos Aires, Buffalo, Brookings, Calcutta, Canton, Cape Cod, Capetown, Cayman Islands, Columbus, Corpus Christi, Dallas, Daytona Beach, Des Moines, Fargo, Flint, Ft. Lauderdale, Frankfurt, Greenwich, Great Falls, Hanoi, Hartford, Havana, Houston, Jersey City, Knoxville, La Paz, Lincoln, London, Lowell, Lynchburg, Lodi, Madrid, Mason City, Memphis, Mexico City, Miami, Mobile, Muncie, New

Brunswick, New Haven, New Orleans, New York, Omaha, Paris, Pasadena, Philadelphia, Reading, Reno, Saginaw, Saigon, San Diego, San Jose, Seoul, South Bend, Spokane, Sydney, Tallahassee, Tillamook, Toronto, Tucson, Utica, Vancouver, Virginia Beach, Warsaw, Washington, D.C., Wheeling, Youngstown, Zurich

Foreign Shores

- Egypt, French Riviera, India, Israel, Prince Edward Island, Turkey

Harmonious Locations:

- Africa, Antigua, Caan, France, Germany, Greece, Guatemala,. Italy, France, Newfoundland, Nova Scotia, Ontario, Palestine, Panama, Portugal, Sao Paulo, Scotland, South America, St. Thomas, St. Vincent, Sweden, Switzerland, Tibet

Anchor Points

United States

- Colorado. Florida, Kansas, Kentucky, Louisiana, Minnesota, Nevada, Oregon

Harmonious Locations:

- Alabama, California, Connecticut, Idaho, Indiana, Maryland, Michigan, Mississippi, New Hampshire, New Jersey, North Carolina, North Dakota, Oklahoma, Rhode Island, Tennessee, Washington, Wyoming

Cities Worldwide

- Bakersfield, Buenos Aires, Brookings, Cape Cod, Fargo, Frankfurt, Greenwich, Great Falls, La Paz, London, Lynchburg, Mason City, Memphis, Mobile, Muncie, New Haven, Omaha, Philadelphia, Saginaw, Saigon, San Diego, San Jose, Sydney, Tucson, Wheeling, Youngstown

Harmonious Locations:

- Akron, Alexandria, Amsterdam, Anaheim, Atlanta, Baltimore, Berlin, Birmingham, Bombay, Boston, Bridgeport, Caan, Canton, Capetown, Charleston, Chicago, Cincinnati, Columbus, Corpus Christi, Dallas, Denver, Des Moines, Flint, Frankfurt, Fresno, Houston, Jersey City, Kingman, Lincoln, Lodi, Los Angeles,

Louisville, Lowell, Macon, Madrid, Mecca, Modesto, Moscow, Naples, Oklahoma City, Orlando, Oslo, Reading, Reno, Rio de Janeiro, Rome, Salem, Sao Paulo, San Antonio, San Francisco, Scranton, Tacoma, Tallahassee, Tampa, Topeka, Tokyo, Trenton, Valencia, Vancouver, Warsaw, Waterbury, Zurich

Foreign Shores

• Africa, Antigua, Germany, France, Nova Scotia, Ontario, Palestine, Portugal, St. Thomas, St. Vincent

Harmonious Locations:

• Ankara, Addis Ababa, Aruba, Belgium, Canada, Egypt, French Riviera, Greece, India, Iran, Israel, Italy, Japan, Mexico, Newfoundland, New Zealand, Norway, Panama, Peru, Prince Edward Island, Scotland, South America, Sweden, Switzerland, Turkey, Wales

Anchor Points

United States
- Arizona, Arkansas, Catalina Island, Iowa, New Mexico, New York, South Carolina

Harmonious Locations:
- Alaska, Cincinnati, Delaware, Hawaii, Illinois, Maine, Massachusetts, Montana, South Dakota, Texas

Cities Worldwide
- Battle Creek, Billings, Buffalo, Charlotte, Eugene, Grand Rapids, Hollywood, Nashville, New York, Providence, Rochester, Salt Lake City, Staten Island, Syracuse

Harmonious Locations:
- Augusta, Amarillo, Anaheim, Anchorage, Atlanta, Berlin, Bridgeport, Calcutta, Cincinnati, Daytona Beach, Hartford, Mexico City, Miami, Montego Bay, New Orleans, Paris, Rio de Janeiro, Rome, Sao Paulo, Santo Domingo, Seoul, South Bend, Spokane, Stamford, Staten Island, Tampa, Tangiers, Tillamook, Toronto, Utica, Virginia Beach

Foreign Shores
- Australia, Denmark, England, Holland, Manitoba, Vietnam

Harmonious Locations:

- Belgium, Canada, Cayman Islands, Cuba, Gambia, Iran, Ireland, Japan, New Brunswick, New Zealand, Norway, Paradise Island, Peru, Syria, Wales

Anchor Points

Born on the 4th, 13th, 22th or 31st

United States

- Alabama, Mississippi, New Hampshire, North Carolina, Oklahoma, Washington

Harmonious Locations:

- California, Colorado, Connecticut, Florida, Idaho, Indiana, Kansas, Kentucky, Louisiana, Maryland, Michigan, Minnesota, Nevada, New Jersey, North Dakota, Oregon, Rhode Island, Tennessee, Wyoming, Utah

Cities Worldwide

- Amsterdam, Birmingham, Bombay, Boston, Canton, Dallas, Des Moines, Houston, Jersey City, Lodi, Madrid, Reading, Tallahassee, Vancouver, Warsaw, Zurich

Harmonious Locations:

- Albany, Albuquerque, Akron, Alexandria, Amsterdam, Arlington, Atlantic City, Baltimore, Caan, Cairo, Cape Cod, Capetown, Chicago, Columbus, Corpus Christi, Dayton, Dhaka, Denver, Detroit, Durham, Erie, Flint, Fresno, Hong Kong, Jackson, Jacksonville, Jerusalem, Las Vegas, Laredo, Kansas City, Lincoln, London, Los Angeles, Louisville, Lowell, Mecca, Milwaukee, Minneapolis, Mobile, Modesto, Moscow, Oklahoma City, Orlando,

Oslo, Pensacola, Pittsburgh, Portland, Provo, Reno, Sacramento, Salem, Sao Paulo, San Diego, Saratoga, San Antonio, San Francisco, Scranton, Scottsdale, Simi Valley, Spokane, Tacoma, Topeka, Tokyo, Trenton, Trinidad, Tulsa, Washington, D.C.

Foreign Shores

• Italy

Harmonious Locations:

• Anguilla, Belize, French Riviera, Greece, India, Israel, Korea, Newfoundland, Nova Scotia, Ontario, Portugal, Prince Edward Island, Scotland, South America, Spain, Sweden, Switzerland, Trinidad, Turkey

Anchor Points

United States

- Utah

Harmonious Locations:

- Any state except: Arizona, Arkansas, Iowa, New Mexico, New York, South Carolina, Delaware, Hawaii, Maine, Minnesota, Montana, Texas

Cities Worldwide

- Akron, Albuquerque, Baltimore. Chicago, Denver, Fresno, Jerusalem, Kansas City, Las Vegas, Pensacola, Pittsburgh, Provo, Salem, San Antonio, San Francisco, Scranton, Topeka, Tokyo

Harmonious Locations:

- Acapulco, Akron, Alexandria, Amarillo, Amsterdam, Anaheim, Anchorage, Anguilla, Athens, Atlanta, Asheville, Attica, Augusta, Bakersfield, Bangkok, Buenos Aires, Buffalo, Brookings, Caan, Cairo, Calcutta, Canton, Cape Cod, Capetown, Casablanca, Chicago, Columbus, Corpus Christi, Curacao, Baltimore, Berlin, Birmingham, Bombay, Boston, Bridgeport, Chicago, Cincinnati, Dallas, Daytona Beach, Denver, Des Moines, Detroit, Fargo, Flint, Frankfurt, Fresno, Great Falls, Greensboro, Greenwich, Hamburg, Hartford, Hicksville, Hong Kong, Houston, Huntsville, Jacksonville,

Jersey City, Jerusalem, Kansas City, La Paz, Lincoln, Lodi, London, Los Angeles, Louisville, Lowell, Lynchburg, Madrid, Mason City, Mecca, Memphis, Mexico City, Miami, Milan, Milwaukee, Minneapolis, Mobile, Moscow, Muncie, New Haven, New Orleans, Nice, Oakland, Oklahoma City, Omaha, Orlando, Osaka, Oslo, Palm Beach, Paris, Pensacola, Philadelphia, Pittsburgh, Portland, Provo, Reading, Reno, Rio de Janeiro, Rome, Saginaw, Saigon, Salem, San Diego, San Jose, San Antonio, Sacramento, San Francisco, Santa Cruz, Sao Paulo, Scranton, Scottsdale, Seattle, Seoul, Simi Valley, South Bend, Spokane, St. Croix, Stockholm, Sydney, Tacoma, Tallahassee, Tampa, Tillamook, Topeka, Toronto, Trenton, Tucson, Tulsa, Vancouver, Utica, Vienna, Virginia Beach, Warsaw, Wheeling, Youngstown, Zurich

Foreign Shores

• Alberta, Anguilla, Belize, Korea, Spain

Harmonious Locations:

• Africa, Antigua, Aruba, Belgium, Canada, Cayman Islands, China, Egypt, France, French Riviera, Germany, Greece, India, Iran, Ireland, Israel, Italy, Japan, Mexico, Newfoundland, New Brunswick, New Zealand, Norway, Nova Scotia, Palestine, Peru, Portugal, Prince Edward Island, Scotland, South America, St. Thomas, St. Vincent, Sweden, Switzerland, Syria, Tibet, Turkey, Wales

Anchor Points

United States

* Delaware, Hawaii, Maine, Massachusetts, Montana, Texas

Harmonious Locations:

* Alaska, Arizona, Arkansas, Colorado, Florida, Illinois, Iowa, Kansas, Kentucky, Louisiana, Mexico, Minnesota, Nevada, New York, Oregon, South Carolina, South Dakota

Cities Worldwide

* Anaheim, Atlanta, Berlin, Bridgeport, Cincinnati, Rio de Janeiro, Rome, Tampa

Harmonious Locations:

* Amarillo, Anchorage, Augusta, Bakersfield, Battle Creek, Billings, Buenos Aires, Buffalo, Brookings, Calcutta, Catalina Island, Charlotte, Daytona Beach, Eugene, Fargo, Frankfurt, Grand Rapids, Greenwich, Great Falls, Hartford, Hollywood, La Paz, London, Lynchburg, Mason City, Memphis, Mexico City, Mobile, Muncie, Nashville, New Haven, New Orleans, New York, Omaha, Paris, Philadelphia, Providence, Rochester, Saginaw, Saigon, Salt Lake City, San Jose, Seoul, South Bend, Spokane, Staten Island, Sydney, Syracuse, Tillamook, Toronto, Tucson, Utica, Wheeling, Youngstown

Foreign Shores

- Belgium, Canada, Iran, Japan, Mexico, New Zealand, Norway, Peru, Wales

Harmonious Locations:

- Africa, Antigua, Australia, Denmark, England, France, Germany, Holland, Ireland, Manitoba, New Brunswick, Palestine, St. Thomas, St. Vincent, Syria, Vietnam

Anchor Points

United States

- California, Indiana, Maryland, New Jersey, Tennessee, Wyoming

Harmonious Locations:

- Alabama, Colorado, Connecticut, Florida, Idaho, Kansas, Kentucky, Louisiana, Michigan, Minnesota, Mississippi, Nevada, New Hampshire, North Carolina, North Dakota, Oklahoma, Oregon, Rhode Island, Washington

Cities Worldwide

- Capetown, Columbus, Corpus Christi, Flint, Lincoln, Lowell

Harmonious Locations:

- Amsterdam, Bakersfield, Birmingham, Bombay, Boston, Buenos Aires, Brookings, Caan, Cairo, Canton, Cape Cod, Chicago, Dallas, Des Moines, Detroit, Fargo, Frankfurt, Greenwich, Great Falls, Hong Kong, Houston, Jersey City, La Paz, Lodi, Los Angeles, London, Louisville, Lynchburg, Madrid, Mason City, Memphis, Milwaukee, Minneapolis, Mobile, Modesto, Muncie, Naples, New Haven, Omaha, Philadelphia, Portland, Reading, Sacramento, Saginaw, Saigon, San Diego, San Jose, Sao Paulo, Scottsdale, Simi Valley, Sydney, Tallahassee, Tucson, Tulsa, Valencia, Vancouver, Warsaw, Wheeling, Youngstown

Foreign Shores

- Scotland, South America, Sweden, Switzerland

Harmonious Locations:

- Africa, Antigua, Egypt, French Riviera, Germany, France, India, Israel, Italy, Nova Scotia, Ontario, Palestine, Portugal, Prince Edward Island, St. Thomas, St. Vincent, Turkey

Anchor Points

United States

- Delaware, Hawaii, Maine, Massachusetts, Montana, Texas

Harmonious Locations:

- Arizona, Arkansas, Delaware, Hawaii, Iowa, Maine, Massachusetts, Montana, New Mexico, New York, South Carolina, Texas

Cities Worldwide

- Anaheim, Atlanta, Bridgeport, Cincinnati, Cleveland, Dublin, Johannesburg, Montreal, Oak Harbor, Peking, Raleigh, Stamford, Stockholm, Tampa, Teheran

Harmonious Locations:

- Anaheim, Atlanta, Battle Creek, Berlin, Billings, Bridgeport, Buffalo, Charlotte, Cincinnati, Eugene, Grand Rapids, Hollywood, Nashville, New York, Providence, Rio de Janeiro, Rochester, Rome, Salt Lake City, Staten Island, Syracuse, Tampa, Waco

Foreign Shores

- Austria, British Columbia, China, Greenland, Montreal, Quebec

Harmonious Locations:

- Australia, Belgium, Canada, Catalina Island, Delaware, Denmark, England, Hawaii, Holland, Iran, Japan, Maine, Manitoba, Massachusetts, Mexico, Montana, New Zealand, Norway, Peru, Vietnam, Wales

Anchor Points

United States

- Alaska, Illinois, South Dakota

Harmonious Locations:

- Arizona, Arkansas, Connecticut, Delaware, Hawaii, Idaho, Iowa, Maine, Massachusetts, Michigan, Montana, New Mexico, New York, North Dakota, Rhode Island, South Carolina, Texas

Cities Worldwide

- Amarillo, Anchorage, Augusta, Buffalo, Calcutta, Daytona Beach, Hartford, Mexico City, Miami, New Orleans, Paris, Seoul, South Bend, Spokane, Tillamook, Toronto, Utica, Virginia Beach

Harmonious Locations:

- Amsterdam, Anaheim, Antigua, Atlanta, Battle Creek, Berlin, Bridgeport, Caan, Cairo, Charlotte, Chicago, Cincinnati, Detroit, Eugene, Grand Rapids, Hollywood, Hong Kong, Los Angeles, Louisville, Milwaukee, Minneapolis, Nashville, New York, Portland, Providence, Rio de Janeiro, Rochester, Rome, Sacramento, Sao Paulo, Salt Lake City, Scottsdale, Seattle, Simi Valley, Staten Island, Syracuse, Tampa, Tulsa,

Foreign Shores

- Cayman Islands, Ireland, New Brunswick, Syria

Harmonious Locations:

- Australia, Belgium, Canada, Catalina Island, Denmark, Egypt, England, French Riviera, Holland, India, Iran, Israel, Japan, Manitoba, Mexico, New Zealand, Norway, Peru, Prince Edward Island, Sweden, Turkey, Vietnam, Wales

Astrological Influences

Astrological Influences and How They Work

As we navigate our personal Port of Call from January 1st to December 31st, we also ride the waves of our Astrological Influence (AI) from one birthday to another. Unlike our personal year, which is different for each of us, the AI is the same for all us at the same age, and journeys through a cycle of twelve—one for each house of the zodiac.

Find your age on Table 23, then look in the AI column to the left to determine the astrological influence you are currently touring.

Table 23. AI—The Age When It Occurs

AI	Age When It Occurs						
1	0	12,	24,	36,	48,	60,	72	84
12	1	13,	25,	37,	49,	61,	73,	85
11	2	14,	26,	38,	50,	62,	74,	86
10	3	15,	27,	39,	51,	63,	75,	87
9	4	16,	28,	40,	52,	64,	76,	88
8	5	17,	29,	41,	53,	65,	77,	89
7	6	18,	30,	42,	54,	66,	78,	90
6	7	19,	31,	43,	55,	67,	79,	91
5	8	20,	32,	44,	56,	68,	80,	92
4	9,	21,	33,	45,	57,	69,	81,	93
3	10,	22,	34,	46,	58,	70,	82,	94
2	11,	23,	35,	47,	59,	71,	83,	95

How to Combine Your Personal Year (Port) With Your Astrological Influence (AI)

If your birthday falls in January, your Port of Call and your astrological influence will run parallel for the entire year. If your birthday falls in any other month, your astrological influence will overlap two different personal years. You will need to check Table 23 on or around your birthday to explore your new astrological influence and see what is on the horizon.

For Example:

Heidi is 31, her birthday is August 12th, and she is currently touring her #6 Port of call. From her 31st birthday on August 12, 2001, until her 32nd birthday on August 12, 2002, Heidi's AI is #6. See Table 29, AI Chart #6, Port 6/AI 6 to reveal more detailed specifics regarding her yearly outcome. For example:

AI Chart #6 (See Table 29)
Astrological Influences #1 through 12
with Port of Call #6

Port	AI	Outcome
6	6	The focus is on your family, especially concerning their health and well being. If you are planning to add to your family, you may be getting into shape to get "out of shape".

Because Heidi's birthday falls in a month other than January, her personal year will overlap two different astrological influences.

From her 32nd birthday on August 12, 2002, until her 33rd birthday on August 12, 2003, Heidi's AI is #5, so she should read Table 29, AI Chart #6, Port 6/AI 5 for her outcome for the remainder of the year. For example:

AI Chart #6 (See Table 29)
Astrological Influences #1 through 12
with Port of Call #5

Port	AI	Outcome
6	5	The tide is leaning towards marriage and tide pools may bring new tadpoles. Marriage proposals are in the winds, and pregnancies are eminent. Whether you are married or single, love is in the air.

Go now and see what your personal Port of Call and your astrological influences will bring you this year. Then look ahead to see what the winds of change create for you in the future.

> Forget not that the earth delights to feel
> your bare feet and the winds long to
> play with your hair.
> —Kahlil Gibran

Table 24. AI Chart #1
Astrological Influences #1—12 with Port of Call #1

Port	AI	Combined Influence
1	1	You set sail on an "I —Me—My" course this year with total focus on yourself. Your journey will take you inward to work on your emotional and mental attitudes, and then outward to tackle your physical appearance and get in ship shape. You will put yourself before others and choose not to let anyone rock your boat. This is your chance to chart your course and sail where you want regardless of what others say or do.
1	2	If your financial picture has been keeping you below deck, the purser is about to pay off as you put your financial house in order. Your sense of security and confidence improve as you become more independent and spend more time topside.
1	3	Independence could come from buying a new vessel or a different car. If you've been carpooling, you may decide to go it alone. You might even take a short trip or two by yourself. You could also find yourself feeling detached from siblings and other relatives and their opinions, but may also be asked to man the deck or steer the ship.
1	4	You could find yourself buying or selling property. If you've been living with parents or roommates, you may decide to live alone and assert your independence.
1	5	You might find yourself exerting your independence by playing the stock market or taking chances at the roulette wheel. There will be ample opportunities for advancement. You'll be filled with new ideas, especially those that show off your creative side. Although you may not have as much time to spend with your love this year, the time you do spend should be romantic.
1	6	The 6th AI deals with daily routine, work, and tasks to be done. Whether you are the Purser or a Steward, expect your routine to change. This influence also rules health and the conscious mind, and you strive for a more positive attitude and begin a new diet and exercise program.
1	7	You may have difficulty getting together with loved ones this year. Maybe they are spending too much time in the galley and you're spending all your time on deck. Getting in touch with yourself is paramount, and partnerships will often be put on the back burner as you stress the need to work independently of others.
1	8	The 8th AI represents new life chapters, rebirth, and regeneration, and the number 1 represents the self and independence, so you can expect to sail into unknown territory and experience new adventures that help create a brand new you.
1	9	You engage in long-distance travel this year, and your journey could take you to foreign shores. This is a great year to learn a foreign language, since the 9th AI covers academia, higher learning and foreigners; and you might be taking an independent stand on moral and ethical issues.
1	10	You might be thinking of sailing your ship alone or map a brand new journey. This is the year to do it. The 10th AI deals with your career, and the number 1 relates to you and your independence. You could find yourself starting a new career, getting a new job, or being promoted. Chart your course and see where the current of life takes you!
1	11	Dare to think about your own personal hopes, wishes and dreams. This is the year where your treasure map pays off and the bounty is yours. You may find yourself spending lots of time with the crew or other groups, even though your desire is to be positioned in the Crow's Nest or spending time alone on your own personal island.
1	12	This is a year where you may have to stand alone against pirates and other hidden enemies (if you have them). Because the number 1 has to do with the self, and the 12th AI has to do with self-sacrifice, you could find yourself confined due to someone else's SOS.

Port: See Tables 1 through 11 to determine your personal Port of Call for the current year.
AI: See Table 23 to find your astrological influence for your current age.

Table 25. AI Chart #2
Astrological Influences #1—12 with Port of Call #2

Port	AI	Combined Influence
2	1	You may have difficulty making headway at times, and will feel you've been anchored long enough—especially with matters that concern you and what you want. You want to be independent, but cooperation is the key. Swallow your pride and ask the crew for help.
2	2	The focus is on money, and you may have to wait for your bounty. When you get it, you could find yourself spending it on the women in your life. This is a good year to untangle your finances so you can stay afloat.
2	3	This year brings a wake of communication with brothers and sisters, and especially the women in your life. You may find yourself moving the rudder back and forth in an attempt to sail forward, and patience is the key. Or you could find yourself trading in your craft for something bigger, better, bolder.
2	4	You could find yourself drawing closer to the women in your life—such as your mother, sisters, friends, aunts, cousins and co-workers. You may choose to stay on dry land rather than be adrift this year as you attend to your environment and property matters.
2	5	You'll have plenty of opportunities to increase your bounty and show off your tacking skills You could also find a very satisfying love relationship this year among the buoys and gulls.
2	6	Delays due to health issues can slow you down and delay your progress. For women, this could mean dealing with female oriented health issues. Plan plenty of time for rest and relaxation and don't let petty annoyances zap your energy.
2	7	This year your explorations focus on marriage and partnerships of all kinds, and your journey will teach you cooperation and patience on a very deep level.
2	8	Your patience and cooperation pays off for you. Perhaps you discover a treasure chest, or inherit more than a few Pieces of Eight. At the very least, you'll be able to borrow a large number of pesos.
2	9	You could find yourself sailing off into the sunset to an out-of-the-way inlet with someone you really care about. Try not to let those pesky little legal problems distract you and pull you off course.
2	10	Financial winds blow steady, and the year may be slow moving. Changes in career may be put on hold, and tact and diplomacy are definitely required in the workplace this year—especially with women.
2	11	Your journey will lead you to a network of people who will help you learn patience and cooperation and a friend could come aboard to help you with a special project. To add to your pleasure, you could make a dream or two come true while you're at it.
2	12	Your journey may take you to the bedside of an ailing friend or relative (especially females). Be careful how you steer your ship so that you don't find yourself in sick bay. Sensitive issues must be handled with discretion, so as not to stir up trouble from hidden enemies.

Port: See Tables 1 through 11 to determine your personal Port of Call for the current year.
AI: See Table 23 to find your astrological influence for your current age.

Table 26. AI Chart #3
Astrological Influences #1—12 with Port of Call #1

Port	Astro	Combined Influence
3	1	Lots of social events and celebrations are on the horizon, and you may decide to host a wave of events yourself. You'll find yourself surrounded by lots of friends and family, but will be preoccupied with sailing away to places unknown.
3	2	You channel your talents and abilities this year, and may find yourself working two jobs at times in order to add more money to your treasure chest. It's o.k. to moonlight; just don't quit your day job.
3	3	You will drop anchor in lots of different places this year, as your social life picks up. Tack carefully, though, to avoid triangles and "he said/she said" situations. This is a very social year for you, and many opportunities could come to you through friends and family. This year centers around communications of all types—written, spoken, visual, audio, etc.
3	4	You may decide to buy or sell property, and this is an excellent time to do that. Plan to spend lots of time in the galley, as your social calendar includes lots of time with friends and family—especially with parents.
3	5	You will have lots of opportunities to improve your talents and abilities or simply just to show them off. You could meet someone at a social gathering, but be careful not to get caught in the undertow of a love triangle. Creativity flows naturally this year, so take advantage of all ideas.
3	6	Social activities will become part of your daily routine this year, and you will probably be more involved socially with your co-workers. Remember to drop anchor regularly to exercise and pay attention to your daily diet to avoid health problems.
3	7	Your marriage or commitment will require clear and direct communication this year. You could find yourself in stormy waters due to competition in your love relationships. You could find yourself being involved with someone who is already involved with someone else, or find yourself in competitive situations with friends, relatives and co-workers.
3	8	This year you have a passport to receive windfalls of money and to make some of your wishes come true. Windfalls can come through prizes, contests and lotteries, inheritance, etc., or you could negotiate a sizeable loan or venture capital to start a private or commercial venture. This is no time to batten down the hatches. Move full steam ahead to advertise and promote.
3	9	Make sure your passport is up to date, as you may find yourself doing a lot of long-distance travel. This year the focus is on international communication, foreigners and foreign languages. At the very least, you will find yourself in some interesting discussions about philosophy, education, publishing and law.
3	10	You could find yourself competing with others in career-oriented situations, or perhaps you'll become involved in a relationship with someone you work with. A lot of your social activity this year will be centered around your career and social status.
3	11	Tailwinds bring you lots of luck this year. Make a wish list and keep it close by, as you will have many chances to make some of your dreams come true. Plan on lots of social activities, especially in groups, as this is an excellent year for communication with friends, relatives and co-workers.
3	12	Competitive situations can throw you off course, because you won't know who is for you and who is against you. Love triangles can cause your boat to capsize, so you would be better off not taking the bait when it's offered.

Port: See Tables 1 through 11 to determine your personal Port of Call for the current year.
AI: See Table 23 to find your astrological influence for your current age.

Table 27. AI Chart #4
Astrological Influences #1—12 with Port of Call #4

Port	AI	Combined Influence
4	1	You could find yourself working hard on something you really want to do, but may be flooded with limitations and restrictions in the process. In some cases, you might just find out that you are your own best friend.
4	2	You work hard this year to bring your financial house in order. You limit your spending and try to stick with a budget to increase your bounty.
4	3	You will find yourself spending more time at work, leaving little time for leisure exploration. Your focus is on stabilizing your security, but don't spend so much time swabbing the deck that you forget to nurture friendships and loveships.
4	4	Even though you may be working from sun up to sundown, you may be flooded with thoughts of moving, and this is an excellent year to sell property. Your home and where you live become your main focus, and you may find yourself drifting back to your early years while pondering the beginnings and endings of life.
4	5	Friendships formed this year may last a lifetime, and for those who are single, a friendship could turn into loveship. If you are looking for love, work may be the best place to find it. This is a year of limitation and restriction, so try to go with the flow. Exercise caution and pay attention to detail. Working hard pays off for you, although you may not always feel appreciated. Don't worry, there will be lots of opportunities available to show off your talents and abilities.
4	6	Get your annual physical and don't put off dental check-ups. Health problems can definitely cause physical limitations and restrictions this year, so make sure you find lots of resting points along the way.
4	7	The focus is on marriage and partnerships of all kinds, but especially those involving friendships. You could end up married to your best friend—or you could feel limited and restricted in your relationship. Legal issues could also be on the horizon, so read the small print on any contracts or documents that are legally binding.
4	8	Limitations and restrictions regarding money could come ashore, but you'll have the power to work it out. You could also come into a sum of money from a legal settlement or situation. Physical limitations or injuries may have to be resolved with surgery.
4	9	Legal problems can be settled in your favor, but there may be limitations and restrictions along the way. Plans to continue or finish higher education can keep your nose to the grind stone and won't leave you much time for stargazing.
4	10	This is a hard-work year, as you strive to get ahead. You may find yourself working long hours and might have to cancel leisure plans to stay on top of things, but in the long run, you could reach and even surpass your goals.
4	11	You tend to navigate in groups this year; people you meet could become some of your closest friends, and some of them will be in your life forever. Chart your course to achieve your goals, and some of your hopes, wishes and dreams will be granted along the way.
4	12	You can't get away with anything this year. Sailing into the wrong place at the wrong time, or trying to get away with something that falls short of the law could land you into trouble—and even in the brig. This influence can bring you physical, mental, and emotional limitations and restrictions, so guard your health and all your activities.

Port: See Tables 1 through 11 to determine your personal Port of Call for the current year.

AI: See Table 23 to find your astrological influence for your current age.

Table 28. AI Chart #5
Astrological Influences #1—12 with Port of Call #5

Port	AI	Combined Influence
5	1	Getting into ship shape will be foremost on your mind, as you embark on making changes in your personal life, your attitudes and your outward appearance.
5	2	You will focus on getting your financial house in order, but expect your bounty to fluctuate up and down a lot this year as you ride the waves of change.
5	3	You may decide to move to a new port of call. While you are looking for a new home, you might decide to navigate with a new car as well.
5	4	The focus is on buying and selling real estate, or making major changes in your environment (where you live and how you live). You'll find yourself torn between staying cozy in your own cove and exploring faraway places.
5	5	Change is definitely on the horizon. You will have lots of opportunities to use your talents and abilities and could possibly move and change jobs this year.
5	6	You will embark on a journey to improve your health and will probably launch a new exercise program. This year is about your health and diet, and changes will be made whether you want them or not. It is best not to take physical risks this year. Slow down and pay attention.
5	7	Those of you who are single may make a sudden decision to plunge into matrimony or may move because of marriage. If already married, you may see lots of changes in your relationship this year. This is definitely a year to spend a lot of time under the moon and stars with the one you love. Love is not the only focus—some of you might decide to make changes in partnerships, or changes in legal documents, or open up a new branch of your business.
5	8	This year could bring changes in joint finances or money you make in conjunction with others. Or perhaps you'll receive an inheritance—cash and property. No matter what your financial picture looks like, expect it to change from day-to-day. There could also be health issues that require surgery.
5	9	You may cast off for places unknown near and far all year long. You may even decide to pack up your loot, say bon voyage to friends and family, and anchor in a new town, a new state, or even another country. Whatever you plan, expect the unexpected, especially when it comes to traveling.
5	10	You may decide to change jobs or launch a new career this year. At the very least, you may find yourself in the same job but in a different place. There will be an undercurrent of change surrounding your career all year long, and you might be logging a lot more travel time as well.
5	11	Changes in career and social status are on the horizon, and you may have a whole new list of hopes, wishes and dreams. You may become involved in new groups and may end up with a few more friends by year's end.
5	12	Waves of activity may cause you to be preoccupied. Pay attention to detail and take your time. Navigate carefully to avoid accidents and hospitals; and if you're going to walk around in the house in the dark, pick up your toys.

Port: See Tables 1 through 11 to determine your personal Port of Call for the current year.
AI: See Table 23 to find your astrological influence for your current age.

Table 29. AI Chart #6
Astrological Influences #1—12 with Port of Call #6

Port	AI	Combined Influence
6	1	Family and domestic responsibilities are on the horizon, while you explore your own personal needs and desires.
6	2	You may be spending more money on weddings and babies this year, either for yourself or for others. Family finances come to the surface, as you chart your course for the future.
6	3	You may need to make a new sign…"baby on board." Many people add new additions to their family under this influence, and sometimes their siblings will follow suit. In addition to a new car seat, you may decide to buy a bigger car as well.
6	4	The focus is on family and drawing closer to or dealing with issues surrounding your mother or motherhood in general. You could decide to buy a home or remodel your existing home.
6	5	The tide is leaning towards marriage and tide pools may bring new tadpoles. Marriage proposals are in the winds, and pregnancies are eminent. Whether you are married or single, love is in the air.
6	6	This year centers around family, especially concerning their health and well being. If you are planning to add to your family, you may be getting into shape to get "out of shape."
6	7	The focus is definitely on love and marriage and you could sail off into the sunset with the person of your dreams. Married or single, this year finds you spending more time with your favorite shipmate.
6	8	You may be discussing joint finances with your mate, or you might get news about an inheritance. You may decide to work on your own legacy as you decide who you want to inherit your treasures.
6	9	Reunions with family and friends take place this year. You may even decide to break down barriers and reconcile your differences with others. You might venture far from home to visit family and friends. Legal issues may also be on the agenda—a marriage license, wills, deeds of trust, divorce decree, etc.
6	10	This year finds you wanting to stick closer to home and spend more time with friends and family, but your boss has you flooded with too much work. Maybe it's time to think about that home-based business you've always wanted. For those who are single, you could meet your future mate through your career or someone you work with.
6	11	This is a year where you could experience domestic bliss—a marriage or pregnancy could make your dreams come true.
6	12	Marriage and family are the focus, and you may have to visit one or more of them in a hospital setting this year. The 12th AI deals with secret enemies, and you may find out that some of them live in your family tree.

Port: See Tables 1 through 11 to determine your personal Port of Call for the current year.
AI: See Table 23 to find your astrological influence for your current age.

Table 30. AI Chart #7
Astrological Influences #1—12 with Port of Call #7

Port	AI	Combined Influence
7	1	This year finds you wanting to pick up anchor and sail away from everything and everyone. This will be a year that is all about you and what you want. You will be thinking about your future and charting your course. You will analyze everything about your life—past, present and future.
7	2	Winds of intrigue surround you as you count your loot and keep your financial picture hidden from the outside world. You may consult a financial counselor or study the stock market in order to get your financial house back on track.
7	3	This year is definitely about secrets and you may keep a few of your own and hold a lot for others. You may also decide to go into a partnership with one of your siblings, and a new car might be on the horizon as well.
7	4	You may find yourself wanting to spend more time at home instead of on the high seas. Your relationship with your mother could be difficult this year. You may keep secrets from each other, but you could also draw closer together as well.
7	5	You could find yourself in a secret affair or be involved in a relationship that you are not quite ready to share with the world. Whatever the case, you could start out spending time under the stars and end up in stormy waters. Either way, it is a very romantic year with lots of intrigue. You could find yourself researching and analyzing opportunities that seem to come from out of the blue.
7	6	This is a year when the winds subside, you retreat to your own private cove to work on improving your mental, emotional and spiritual health.
7	7	You could just find yourself in a secret partnership with someone, or you could fall for someone who is already attached. Be careful. The undertow may be more than you bargained for and you could find yourself alone without a shipmate.
7	8	The tide is in this year as an inheritance or legal resolution brings you money -- or perhaps you decide to pool your resources and enter into a business venture with a partner. But it's not all business. You may pursue the path of spiritual enlightenment or decide to go back to school.
7	9	You may be flooded with legal issues this year, so keep a detailed log. At times you may be riding the waves in faraway places and may be submerged in study. This is a great year to go back to school, work on your degree, study for a new career, or get your Masters.
7	10	You may find yourself studying, researching, or learning something new regarding your career. You could also be going to school and working at the same time. Whatever your explorations, stop at resting points along the way.
7	11	You'd rather spend time alone than with the whole crew, and you will spend a lot of time analyzing your past, present and future and exploring new hopes, wishes and dreams.
7	12	You may find yourself in a relationship, either professional or personal, that you choose to keep secret. Someone close to you may be keeping secrets from you, or vice-versa. There will be a lot going on behind the scenes, so navigate with care to avoid a mutiny.

Port: See Tables 1 through 11 to determine your personal Port of Call for the current year.
AI: See Table 23 to find your astrological influence for your current age.

Table 31. AI Chart #8
Astrological Influences #1—12 with Port of Call #8

Port	Astro	Combined Influence
8	1	This is your year to spend money on yourself, and you do. Power and charisma come easily to you and you definitely can have it all.
8	2	You bounty increases and you will enjoy counting your loot and putting your financial house in better order.
8	3	More power, more loot – how about new wheels? You will spend money on transportation and cars this year.
8	4	O.K. Power, money, and a new car – this year you focus on real estate and your environment. Why not add a new house to your bounty, or a cozy little vacation bungalow at the beach?
8	5	A love affair with someone affluent is on the horizon. If you are already attached, you have more money to spend on each other. You have the power to get paid well for your talents and abilities and could have many opportunities come your way to better yourself.
8	6	You might decide to embark on a new health regimen, buy exercise equipment or join a gym. If you have health problems, you will have the power to overcome them.
8	7	You could meet someone influential and/or marry into wealth this year, or enter into a joint venture with someone that brings you money. This is a powerful year for marriage and partnership.
8	8	You could come into a lot of power and wealth this year, and connect with people of affluence. You could go through a life-altering event that causes you to experience the fine balance between life and death. This is definitely a year focused around power and wealth, and you could inherit money.
8	9	If you are involved in legal situations, you have the power to win. If you are wanting money to go back to school or get your Masters, you'll have it. If you want to sail off to foreign shores, this is the ideal time.
8	10	A promotion or a sizeable raise is on the horizon. Don't be afraid to make waves on the job, as you have the power to get want you want.
8	11	You have the power to make your hopes, wishes and dreams come true, and will be able to influence your friends and groups of people.
8	12	You have power over your hidden enemies, and power comes to you from behind-the-scenes activities. This is a year to overcome mental and emotional problems that have been haunting you for a long time.

Port: See Tables 1 through 11 to determine your personal Port of Call for the current year.
AI: See Table 23 to find your astrological influence for your current age.

Table 32. AI Chart #9
Astrological Influences #1—12 with Port of Call #9

Port	AI	Combined Influence
9	1	If you've been thinking about going it alone, this could be the year you do it. If bad habits have been barriers for you, this is a good time to let them go.
9	2	If your financial picture has been stormy, you may consult with a financial planner and might need to sign legal documents to improve your money flow—perhaps a loan or even bankruptcy.
9	3	You could travel long distance to visit friends and relatives, and your journey might take you to foreign shores.
9	4	You could sell a piece of property and deal with legal issues this year surrounding real estate—such as buying or selling property, refinancing home loans, a beautiful new yacht, etc.
9	5	You could find yourself doing a lot of traveling for professional and personal purposes. You may find yourself ending a love affair. Wait until the first of the year to start a new one, as this year is about "endings" and next year is about "new beginnings."
9	6	If you have been struggling with health issues, this could be the year where you put them behind you. It's a great year to stop smoking or to break bad habits. You may have to say goodbye to friends or co-workers that you spend time with on a daily basis.
9	7	You could end a marriage or partnership this year, or you could find yourself involved in legal situations. You could also do a lot of long distance traveling, especially to out-of-the-way places. This is a year where stormy waters could keep you on edge, so try to go with the ebb and flow of the tides.
9	8	You could come into money from a legal or contractual situation. You may decide to cast off to foreign shores, and you should have the bounty to do it. You could hear about the loss of someone and could inherit some money.
9	9	You will go through a major cycle of completion this year. You will get rid of anything you don't want, don't need, don't like or don't use anymore. You could get something published, and you could become famous for something you do this year.
9	10	You could end a job you have had for a long time, or could end one career and start another. This is definitely about career changes. Remember, endings come before new beginnings in the current of life and change always brings blessings in the end.
9	11	You could find yourself putting some groups of people and/or friends behind you. Don't worry. When you get rid of, give away or lose something, the universe always replaces it with something better.
9	12	You could experience a lot of endings this year, and may have to deal with hidden enemies and behind-the-scenes activities as well. You will probably address mental and emotional issues that have been haunting you the past few years and may decide to rid yourself of them once and for all.

Port: See Tables 1 through 11 to determine your personal Port of Call for the current year.
AI: See Table 23 to find your astrological influence for your current age.

Medical Astrology
and
Personal Health Cycles

Medical Astrology Could Save Your Life

In the 19th Century, the doctor who suggested and proved that fewer women would die from "childbed fever" if the attending doctors and midwives would wash their hands in a chlorinated lime solution, became an outcast in the medical community and died in an insane asylum. Doctors in ancient China were only paid when their patients got well, and in some districts, doctors were obligated to make restitution if a patient became worse or continued to suffer ill health under his care.

How things have changed since the establishment of the American Medical Association and the modernization of medicine. But is it too much to ask that those doctors who take the "Hippocratic Oath" also respect and follow their founding father's counsel in the practice of medicine?

> *"Touch not with iron that part of the body ruled by the sign the Moon is transiting." (From the diaries of Hippocrates)*

What Did Hippocrates Mean By This?

It means that a doctor should not perform a surgical procedure with a knife (iron) upon a part of the patient's body which is ruled by the astrological sign through which the Moon is moving at the time. The Moon remains in one sign approximately two and a half days and this information can be easily obtained from an Ephemeris, the Farmer's Almanac, Llewellyn's Moon Sign Book, or from an astrologer.

101

According to Hippocrates—and it has been proven time and again—one of three things could happen if surgery is performed at the wrong time: 1. Complications could set in, such as infection; 2. Healing and recuperation can be unusually slow and painful; 3. Death could occur.

Complications and slow recuperation is the most common and death is rare, but the safest choice is to heed the warnings of Hippocrates.

Often people are admitted to the hospital for a common and fairly simple surgical procedure only to expire on the operating table for "unknown causes". There are many cases of children who have tonsils removed while the Moon is transiting Taurus and have suffered from severe infections and long periods of recovery.

Let's face it, most doctors don't have the time or desire to learn astrology and probably don't believe in it anyway. However, you do have the power to control dates and times that you or a loved one has surgery. Ask your doctor for two or three dates and times that he or she is available to do the surgery. Then consult an astrologer or a moon sign book to determine which date would be the safest. To help you further, see Table 33, which lists the astrological signs and the body parts they rule.

For example, if you're going to your stomach stapled, don't do it when the Moon is transiting Cancer. If you're wanting to get rid of those pesky bunions, don't do it when the Moon is in Pisces. If you're having back surgery, avoid the Moon in Leo or Scorpio. Need a little brain surgery? Make sure the Moon is not in Aries.

And finally, if you think this information is foolish or you don't think it's necessary, consider the words of Hippocrates, the Father of Medicine...

> *"He who practices medicine without the benefit of the movement of the stars and planets is a fool."*
>
> *(From the diaries of Hippocrates)*

<u>*Disclaimer:*</u>   *The information contained herein is intended for educational purposes only. These statements have not been evaluated by the Food and Drug Administration. Anyone suffering from any disease, illness or injury should consult with a physician or health practitioner.*

Table 33. Body Parts Affected by Astrological Signs

Astrological Sign	Body Parts Affected
ARIES	Head, Face (except nose), Cerebral Hemispheres of the Brain
TAURUS	Neck, Throat, Larynx, Tonsils, Carotid Arteries, Jugular Vein
GEMINI	Lungs, Thymus, Nerves, Upper Ribs, Shoulders, Arms, Hands, Fingers
CANCER	Breast, Chest, Stomach, Diaphragm, Thoracic Duct, Lymph System
LEO	Heart, Aorta, Back and Spinal Cord
VIRGO	Nervous System, Pancreas, Large and Small Intestines
LIBRA	Kidneys, Equilibrium and Balance, Sometimes the Skin
SCORPIO	Reproductive Organs, Genitals, The Blood, Descending Colon, Rectum, Urethra, Nose, Sometimes the Back
SAGITTARIUS	Thighs, Hips, Femur Bone, Liver, Veins, Sacral Region
CAPRICORN	Teeth, Bones, Kneecaps, Skin
AQUARIUS	Circulatory System, Lower Legs and Ankles, Varicose Veins
PISCES	Feet and Toes, Sometimes the Lungs and Intestines, Entire body system related to "leaks" and the draining of fluids

Personal Health Cycles

It is possible to pinpoint a blueprint for a healthier life by being aware of the health problems associated with a particular number.

Find the calendar day of your birth to reveal when ill health or strain from overwork is most likely to manifest.

Your personal health cycle will tell you what ages to watch for health changes good or bad, and the months every year of your life that you need to guard against ill health.

You will also find a list of susceptible health areas. Please be advised that these are *susceptible* health areas, meaning that based on the day you were born and your sun sign, it is possible that you could have one, all, or possibly none of these health problems sometime during your life time.

In order to get the most out of your personal health cycle, you will want to pay attention to your health more closely when you are at an age that your health could change (good or bad), and in a month that you need to guard against ill health, especially if you are having symptoms related to any of the susceptible health areas listed for your birthday.

Disclaimer: *The information contained herein is intended for informational purposes only. These statements have not been evaluated by the Food and Drug Administration. Anyone suffering from any disease, illness or injury should consult with a physician or health practitioner.*

Health Cycles for January Birthdays

JANUARY 1
Age for health changes:
Month to guard health:
Susceptible health areas:

CAPRICORN
1, 10, 19, 28, 37, 46, 55, 64, 73, 82
January, October, December
Bones, Eye Problems, Headaches, Heart and Circulatory System, High Blood Pressure, Kneecaps, Palpitations, Skin, Teeth

JANUARY 2
Age for health changes:
Month to guard health:
Susceptible health areas:

CAPRICORN
2, 11, 20, 29, 38, 47, 56, 65, 74, 83
January, February, July
Bones, Breasts, Digestive system Disorders, Kneecaps, Lymphatic System Disorders, Ovaries, Skin, Stomach, Sympathetic Nervous System, Synovial Fluids, Teeth

JANUARY 3
Age for health changes:
Month to guard health:
Susceptible health areas:

CAPRICORN
3, 12, 21, 30, 39, 48, 57, 66, 75, 84
February, June, September, December
Bones, Excess Strain to Nervous System, Kneecaps, Liver, Neuritis, Sciatica, Skin, Teeth, Throat

JANUARY 4
Age for health changes:
Month to guard health:
Susceptible health areas:

CAPRICORN
4, 13, 22, 31, 40, 49, 58, 67, 76, 85
January, February, July, August, September
Anemia, Bones, Back and Neck Pains, Cramps and Spasms, Kneecaps, Melancholia, Mental Disorders,

108

Palpitations, Skin, Sudden Nervous Breakdowns, Teeth

JANUARY 5   CAPRICORN
Age for health changes: 5, 14, 23, 32, 41, 50, 59, 68, 77, 86
Month to guard health: June, September, December
Susceptible health areas: All Sense, Perception and Sensory Organs, Bones, Central Nervous System, Insomnia, Kneecaps, Respiratory System, Skin, Teeth, Thyroid

JANUARY 6   CAPRICORN
Age for health changes: 6, 15, 24, 33, 42, 51, 60, 69, 78, 87
Month to guard health: May, October, November
Susceptible health areas: Bones, Kidneys, Kneecaps, Liver, Lumbar Region Disorders, Parathyroid, Teeth, Throat, Skin, Veinous Circulation

JANUARY 7   CAPRICORN
Age for health changes: 7, 16, 25, 34, 43, 52, 61, 70, 79, 88
Month to guard health: January, February, July, August
Susceptible health areas: Bones, Depression from Mental Stress, Kneecaps, Prone to Drug and Alcohol Addiction, Sensitive Skin Conditions, Teeth

JANUARY 8   CAPRICORN
Age for health changes: 8, 17, 26, 35, 44, 53, 62, 71, 80
Month to guard health: January, February, July, December
Susceptible health areas: Bones, Gall Bladder, Headaches, Intestines, Kneecaps, Liver Bile, Rheumatism, Skeletal System, Skin, Spleen, Teeth

JANUARY 9

Age for health changes:
Month to guard health:
Susceptible health areas:

CAPRICORN

9, 18, 27, 36, 45, 54, 63, 72, 81
April, May, October, November
Bones, Chicken Pox, Contagious Diseases, Kidneys, Kneecaps, Measles, Muscular System, Red Corpuscles of the Blood, Skin, Teeth

JANUARY 10

Age for health changes:
Months to guard health:
Susceptible health areas:

CAPRICORN

1, 10, 19, 28, 37, 46, 55, 64, 73, 82
January, October, December
Bones, Eye Problems, Headaches, Heart and Circulatory System, High Blood Pressure, Kneecaps, Palpitations, Skin, Teeth

JANUARY 11

Age for health changes:
Month to guard health:
Susceptible health areas:

CAPRICORN

2, 11, 20, 29, 38, 47, 56, 65, 74, 83
January, February, July
Bones, Breasts, Digestive System Disorders, Kneecaps, Lymphatic System Disorders, Ovaries, Skin, Stomach, Sympathetic Nervous System, Synovial Fluids, Teeth

JANUARY 12

Age for health changes:
Month to guard health:
Susceptible health areas:

CAPRICORN

3, 12, 21, 30, 39, 48, 57, 66, 75, 84
February, June, September, December
Bones, Excess Strain to Nervous System, Kneecaps, Liver, Neuritis, Sciatica, Skin, Teeth, Throat

JANUARY 13
Age for health changes:
Month to guard health:
Susceptible health areas:

CAPRICORN
4, 13, 22, 31, 40, 49, 58, 67, 76, 85
January, February, July, August, September
Anemia, Bones, Back and Neck Pains, Cramps and Spasms, Kneecaps, Melancholia, Mental Disorders, Palpitations, Skin, Sudden Nervous Breakdowns, Teeth

JANUARY 14
Age for health changes:
Month to guard health:
Susceptible health areas:

CAPRICORN
5, 14, 23, 32, 41, 50, 59, 68, 77, 86
June, September, December
All Sense, Perception and Sensory Organs, Bones, Central Nervous System, Insomnia, Kneecaps, Respiratory System, Skin, Teeth, Thyroid

JANUARY 15
Age for health changes:
Month to guard health:
Susceptible health areas:

CAPRICORN
6, 15, 24, 33, 42, 51, 60, 69, 78, 87
May, October, November
Bones, Kidneys, Kneecaps, Liver, Lumbar Region Disorders, Parathyroid, Teeth, Throat, Skin, Veinous Circulation

JANUARY 16
Age for health changes:
Month to guard health:
Susceptible health areas:

CAPRICORN
7, 16, 25, 34, 43, 52, 61, 70, 79, 88
January, February, July, August
Bones, Depression from Mental Stress, Kneecaps, Prone to Drug and Alcohol Addiction, Sensitive Skin Conditions, Teeth

JANUARY 17
Age for health changes:
Month to guard health:
Susceptible health areas:

CAPRICORN
8, 17, 26, 35, 44, 53, 62, 71, 80
January, February, July, December
Bones, Gall Bladder, Headaches, Intestines, Kneecaps, Liver Bile, Rheumatism, Skeletal System, Skin, Spleen, Teeth

JANUARY 18
Age for health changes:
Month to guard health:
Susceptible health areas:

CAPRICORN
9, 18, 27, 36, 45, 54, 63, 72, 81
April, May, October, November
Bones, Chicken Pox, Contagious Diseases, Kidneys, Kneecaps, Measles, Muscular System, Red Corpuscles of the Blood, Skin, Teeth

JANUARY 19
Age for health changes:
Month to guard health:
Susceptible health areas:

CAPRICORN
1, 10, 19, 28, 37, 46, 55, 64, 73, 82
January, October, December
Bones, Eye Problems, Headaches, Heart and Circulatory System, High Blood Pressure, Kneecaps, Palpitations, Skin, Teeth

JANUARY 20
Age for health changes:
Month to guard health:
Susceptible health areas:

AQUARIUS
2, 11, 20, 29, 38, 47, 56, 65, 74, 83
January, February, July
Ankles, Breasts, Circulatory System, Digestive System Disorders, Lower Legs, Lymphatic System Disorders, Ovaries, Stomach, Sympathetic Nervous System, Synovial Fluids, Varicose Veins

JANUARY 21
Age for health changes:
Month to guard health:
Susceptible health areas:

AQUARIUS
3, 12, 21, 30, 39, 48, 57, 66, 75, 84
February, June, September, December
Ankles, Circulatory System, Excess Strain to Nervous System, Liver, Lower Legs, Neuritis, Sciatica, Skin, Throat, Varicose Veins

JANUARY 22
Age for health changes:
Month to guard health:
Susceptible health areas:

AQUARIUS
4, 13, 22, 31, 40, 49, 58, 67, 76, 85
January, February, July, August, September
Anemia, Ankles, Back and Neck Pains, Circulatory System, Cramps and Spasms, Lower Legs, Melancholia, Mental Disorders, Palpitations, Sudden Nervous Breakdowns, Varicose Veins

JANUARY 23
Age for health changes:
Month to guard health:
Susceptible health areas:

AQUARIUS
5, 14, 23, 32, 41, 50, 59, 68, 77, 86
June, September, December
All Sense, Perception and Sensory Organs, Ankles, Central Nervous System, Circulatory System, Insomnia, Lower Legs, Respiratory System, Thyroid, Varicose Veins

JANUARY 24
Age for health changes:
Month to guard health:
Susceptible health areas:

AQUARIUS
6, 15, 24, 33, 42, 51, 60, 69, 78, 87
May, October, November
Ankles, Circulatory System, Kidneys, Liver, Lower Legs, Lumbar Region

Disorders, Parathyroid, Throat, Varicose Veins, Veinous Circulation

JANUARY 25   AQUARIUS
Age for health changes: 7, 16, 25, 34, 43, 52, 61, 70, 79, 88
Month to guard health: January, February, July, August
Susceptible health areas: Ankles, Circulatory System, Depression from Mental Stress, Lower Legs, Prone to Drug and Alcohol Addiction, Varicose Veins

JANUARY 26   AQUARIUS
Age for health changes: 8, 17, 26, 35, 44, 53, 62, 71, 80
Month to guard health: January, February, July, December
Susceptible health areas: Ankles, Circulatory System, Gall Bladder, Headaches, Intestines, Liver Bile, Lower Legs, Rheumatism, Skeletal System, Skin, Spleen, Teeth, Varicose Veins

JANUARY 27   AQUARIUS
Age for health changes: 9, 18, 27, 36, 45, 54, 63, 72, 81
Month to guard health: April, May, October, November
Susceptible health areas: Ankles, Chicken Pox, Circulatory System, Contagious Diseases, Kidneys, Lower Legs, Measles, Muscular System, Red Corpuscles of the Blood, Varicose Veins

JANUARY 28   AQUARIUS
Age for health changes: 1, 10, 19, 28, 37, 46, 55, 64, 73, 82
Months to guard health: January, October, December
Susceptible health areas: Ankles, Eye Problems, Headaches, Heart and Circulatory System, High Blood

Pressure, Lower Legs, Palpitations, Varicose Veins

JANUARY 29

Age for health changes:
Month to guard health:
Susceptible health areas:

AQUARIUS
2, 11, 20, 29, 38, 47, 56, 65, 74, 83
January, February, July
Ankles, Breasts, Circulatory System, Digestive System Disorders, Lower Legs, Lymphatic System Disorders, Ovaries, Stomach, Sympathetic Nervous System, Synovial Fluids, Varicose Veins

JANUARY 30

Age for health changes
Month to guard health:
Susceptible health areas:

AQUARIUS
3, 12, 21, 30, 39, 48, 57, 66, 75, 84
February, June, September, December
Ankles, Circulatory System, Excess Strain to Nervous System, Liver, Lower Legs, Neuritis, Sciatica, Skin, Throat, Varicose Veins

Health Cycles for February Birthdays

FEBRUARY 1
Age for health changes:
Months to guard health:
Susceptible health areas:

AQUARIUS
1, 10, 19, 28, 37, 46, 55, 64, 73, 82
January, October, December
Ankles, Eye Problems, Headaches, Heart and Circulatory System, High Blood Pressure, Lower Legs, Palpitations, Varicose Veins

FEBRUARY 2
Age for health changes:
Month to guard health:
Susceptible health areas:

AQUARIUS
2, 11, 20, 29, 38, 47, 56, 65, 74, 83
January, February, July
Ankles, Breasts, Circulatory System, Digestive System Disorders, Lower Legs, Lymphatic System Disorders, Ovaries, Stomach, Sympathetic Nervous System, Synovial Fluids, Varicose Veins

FEBRUARY 3
Age for health changes:
Month to guard health:
Susceptible health areas:

AQUARIUS
3, 12, 21, 30, 39, 48, 57, 66, 75, 84
February, June, September, December
Ankles, Circulatory System, Excess Strain to Nervous System, Liver, Lower Legs, Neuritis, Sciatica, Skin, Throat, Varicose Veins

FEBRUARY 4
Age for health changes:
Month to guard health:

AQUARIUS
4, 13, 22, 31, 40, 49, 58, 67, 76, 85
January, February, July, August, September

Susceptible health areas: Anemia, Ankles, Back and Neck Pains, Circulatory System, Cramps and Spasms, Lower Legs, Melancholia, Mental Disorders, Palpitations, Sudden Nervous Breakdowns, Varicose Veins

FEBRUARY 5 AQUARIUS
Age for health changes: 5, 14, 23, 32, 41, 50, 59, 68, 77, 86
Month to guard health: June, September, December
Susceptible health areas: All Sense, Perception and Sensory Organs, Ankles, Central Nervous System, Circulatory System, Insomnia, Lower Legs, Respiratory System, Thyroid, Varicose Veins

FEBRUARY 6 AQUARIUS
Age for health changes: 6, 15, 24, 33, 42, 51, 60, 69, 78, 87
Month to guard health: May, October, November
Susceptible health areas: Ankles, Circulatory System, Kidneys, Liver, Lower Legs, Lumbar Region Disorders, Parathyroid, Throat, Varicose Veins, Veinous Circulation

FEBRUARY 7 AQUARIUS
Age for health changes: 7, 16, 25, 34, 43, 52, 61, 70, 79, 88
Month to guard health: January, February, July, August
Susceptible health areas: Ankles, Circulatory System, Depression from Mental Stress, Lower Legs, Prone to Drug or Alcohol Addiction, Sensitive Skin Conditions, Varicose Veins

FEBRUARY 8
Age for health changes:
Month to guard health:
Susceptible health areas:

AQUARIUS
8, 17, 26, 35, 44, 53, 62, 71, 80
January, February, July, December
Ankles, Circulatory System, Gall Bladder, Headaches, Intestines, Liver Bile, Lower Legs, Rheumatism, Skeletal System, Skin, Spleen, Teeth, Varicose Veins

FEBRUARY 9
Age for health changes:
Month to guard health:
Susceptible health areas:

AQUARIUS
9, 18, 27, 36, 45, 54, 63, 72, 81
April, May, October, November
Ankles, Chicken Pox, Circulatory System, Contagious Diseases, Kidneys, Lower Legs, Measles, Muscular System, Red Corpuscles of the Blood, Varicose Veins

FEBRUARY 10
Age for health changes:
Months to guard health:
Susceptible health areas:

AQUARIUS
1, 10, 19, 28, 37, 46, 55, 64, 73, 82
January, October, December
Ankles, Eye Problems, Headaches, Heart and Circulatory System, High Blood Pressure, Lower Legs, Palpitations, Varicose Veins

FEBRUARY 11
Age for health changes:
Month to guard health:
Susceptible health areas:

AQUARIUS
2, 11, 20, 29, 38, 47, 56, 65, 74, 83
January, February, July
Ankles, Breasts, Circulatory System, Digestive System Disorders, Lower Legs, Lymphatic System Disorders, Ovaries, Stomach, Sympathetic Nervous System, Synovial Fluids, Varicose Veins

FEBRUARY 12
Age for health changes:
Month to guard health:
Susceptible health areas:

AQUARIUS
3, 12, 21, 30, 39, 48, 57, 66, 75, 84
February, June, September, December
Ankles, Circulatory System, Excess Strain to Nervous System, Liver, Lower Legs, Neuritis, Sciatica, Skin, Throat, Varicose Veins

FEBRUARY 13
Age for health changes:
Month to guard health:
Susceptible health areas:

AQUARIUS
4, 13, 22, 31, 40, 49, 58, 67, 76, 85
January, February, July, August, September
Anemia, Ankles, Back and Neck Pains, Circulatory System, Cramps and Spasms, Lower Legs, Melancholia, Mental Disorders, Palpitations, Sudden Nervous Breakdowns, Varicose Veins

FEBRUARY 14
Age for health changes:
Month to guard health:
Susceptible health areas:

AQUARIUS
5, 14, 23, 32, 41, 50, 59, 68, 77, 86
June, September, December
All Sense, Perception and Sensory Organs, Ankles, Central Nervous System, Circulatory System, Insomnia, Lower Legs, Respiratory System, Thyroid, Varicose Veins

FEBRUARY 15
Age for health changes:
Month to guard health:
Susceptible health areas:

AQUARIUS
6, 15, 24, 33, 42, 51, 60, 69, 78, 87
May, October, November
Ankles, Circulatory System, Kidneys, Liver, Lower Legs, Lumbar Region

Disorders, Parathyroid, Throat, Varicose Veins, Veinous Circulation

FEBRUARY 16
Age for health changes:
Month to guard health:
Susceptible health areas:

AQUARIUS
7, 16, 25, 34, 43, 52, 61, 70, 79, 88
January, February, July, August
Ankles, Circulatory System, Depression from Mental Stress, Lower Legs, Prone to Drug or Alcohol Addiction, Sensitive Skin Conditions, Varicose Veins

FEBRUARY 17
Age for health changes:
Month to guard health:
Susceptible health areas:

AQUARIUS
8, 17, 26, 35, 44, 53, 62, 71, 80
January, February, July, December
Ankles, Circulatory System, Gall Bladder, Headaches, Intestines, Liver Bile, Lower Legs, Rheumatism, Skeletal System, Skin, Spleen, Teeth, Varicose Veins

FEBRUARY 18
Age for health changes:
Month to guard health:
Susceptible health areas:

AQUARIUS
9, 18, 27, 36, 45, 54, 63, 72, 81
April, May, October, November
Ankles, Chicken Pox, Circulatory System, Contagious Diseases, Kidneys, Lower Legs, Measles, Muscular System, Red Corpuscles of the Blood, Varicose Veins

FEBRUARY 19
Age for health changes:
Months to guard health:
Susceptible health areas:

PISCES
1, 10, 19, 28, 37, 46, 55, 64, 73, 82
January, October, December
Eye Problems, Feet and Toes, Entire Body System related to Leaks" and the Draining

of Fluids, Headaches, Heart and Circulatory System, High Blood Pressure, Palpitations, Sometimes the Lungs and Intestines

FEBRUARY 20	**PISCES**
Age for health changes:	2, 11, 20, 29, 38, 47, 56, 65, 74, 83
Month to guard health:	January, February, July
Susceptible health areas:	Breasts, Digestive System Disorders, Entire Body System related to "Leaks" and the Draining of Fluids, Feet and Toes, Lymphatic System Disorders, Ovaries, Sometimes the Lungs and Intestines, Stomach, Sympathetic Nervous System, Synovial Fluids

FEBRUARY 21	**PISCES**
Age for health changes:	3, 12, 21, 30, 39, 48, 57, 66, 75, 84
Month to guard health:	February, June, September, December
Susceptible health areas:	Entire Body System related to "Leaks" and the Draining of Fluids, Excess Strain to Nervous System, Feet and Toes, Liver, Neuritis, Sciatica, Skin, Sometimes the Lungs and Intestines, Throat

FEBRUARY 22	**PISCES**
Age for health changes:	4, 13, 22, 31, 40, 49, 58, 67, 76, 85
Month to guard health:	January, February, July, August, September
Susceptible health areas:	Anemia, Back and Neck Pains, Cramps and Spasms, Entire Body System related to "Leaks" and the Draining of Fluids, Feet and Toes, Melancholia, Mental Disorders,

Palpitations, Sometimes the Lungs and Intestines, Sudden Nervous Breakdowns

FEBRUARY 23

PISCES

Age for health changes: 5, 14, 23, 32, 41, 50, 59, 68, 77, 86

Month to guard health: June, September, December

Susceptible health areas: All Sense, Perception and Sensory Organs, Central Nervous System, Entire Body System related to "Leaks" and the Draining of Fluids, Feet and Toes, Insomnia, Respiratory System, Sometimes the Lungs and Intestines, Thyroid

FEBRUARY 24

PISCES

Age for health changes: 6, 15, 24, 33, 42, 51, 60, 69, 78, 87

Month to guard health: May, October, November

Susceptible health areas: Entire Body System related to "Leaks" and the Draining of Fluids, Feet and Toes, Kidneys, Liver, Lumbar Region Disorders, Parathyroid, Sometimes the Lungs and Intestines, Throat, Veinous Circulation

FEBRUARY 25

PISCES

Age for health changes: 7, 16, 25, 34, 43, 52, 61, 70, 79, 88

Month to guard health: January, February, July, August

Susceptible health areas: Depression from Mental Stress, Entire Body System related to "Leaks" and the Draining of Fluids, Feet and Toes, Prone to Drug or Alcohol Addiction, Sensitive Skin Conditions, Sometimes the Lungs and Intestines

FEBRUARY 26
Age for health changes:
Month to guard health:
Susceptible health areas:

PISCES
8, 17, 26, 35, 44, 53, 62, 71, 80
January, February, July, December
Entire Body System related to "Leaks" and the Draining of Fluids, Feet and Toes, Gall Bladder, Headaches, Intestines, Liver Bile, Rheumatism, Skeletal System, Skin, Sometimes the Lungs, Spleen, Teeth

FEBRUARY 27
Age for health changes:
Month to guard health:
Susceptible health areas:

PISCES
9, 18, 27, 36, 45, 54, 63, 72, 81
April, May, October, November
Chicken Pox, Contagious Diseases, Entire Body System related to "Leaks" and the Draining of Fluids, Feet and Toes, Kidneys, Measles, Muscular System, Red Corpuscles of the Blood, Sometimes the Lungs and Intestines

FEBRUARY 28
Age for health changes:
Months to guard health:
Susceptible health areas:

PISCES
1, 10, 19, 28, 37, 46, 55, 64, 73, 82
January, October, December
Entire Body System related to "Leaks" and the Draining of Fluids, Eye Problems, Feet and Toes, Headaches, Heart and Circulatory System, High Blood Pressure, Palpitations, Sometimes the Lungs and Intestines

FEBRUARY 29
Age for health changes:

PISCES
2, 11, 20, 29, 38, 47, 56, 65, 74, 83

Month to guard health: January, February, July
Susceptible health areas: Breasts, Digestive System Disorders,
                                Entire Body System related to "Leaks" and
                                the Draining of Fluids, Feet and Toes,
                                Lymphatic System Disorders, Ovaries,
                                Sometimes the Lungs and Intestines,
                                Stomach, Sympathetic Nervous System,
                                Synovial Fluids

Health Cycles for March Birthdays

MARCH 1
Age for health changes:
Months to guard health:
Susceptible health areas:

PISCES
1, 10, 19, 28, 37, 46, 55, 64, 73, 82
January, October, December
Eye Problems, Feet and Toes, Entire Body System related to Leaks" and the Draining of Fluids, Headaches, Heart and Circulatory System, High Blood Pressure, Palpitations, Sometimes the Lungs and Intestines

MARCH 2
Age for health changes:
Months to guard health:
Susceptible health areas:

PISCES
2, 11, 20, 29, 38, 47, 56, 65, 74, 83
January, February, July
Breasts, Digestive System Disorders, Entire Body System related to "Leaks" and the Draining of Fluids, Feet and Toes, Lymphatic System Disorders, Ovaries, Sometimes the Lungs and Intestines, Stomach, Sympathetic Nervous System, Synovial Fluids

MARCH 3
Age for health changes:
Months to guard health:
Susceptible health areas:

PISCES
3, 12, 21, 30, 39, 48, 57, 66, 75, 84
February, June, September, December
Entire Body System related to "Leaks" and the Draining of Fluids, Excess Strain to Nervous System, Feet and Toes, Liver, Neuritis, Sciatica, Skin, Sometimes the Lungs and Intestines, Throat

MARCH 4   PISCES
Age for health changes: 4, 13, 22, 31, 40, 49, 58, 67, 76, 85
Months to guard health: January, February, July, August, September
Susceptible health areas: Anemia, Back and Neck Pains, Cramps
                                    and Spasms, Entire Body System related to
                                    "Leaks" and the Draining of Fluids, Feet
                                    and Toes, Melancholia, Mental Disorders,
                                    Palpitations, Sometimes the Lungs and
                                    Intestines, Sudden Nervous Breakdowns

MARCH 5   PISCES
Age for health changes: 5, 14, 23, 32, 41, 50, 59, 68, 77, 86
Months to guard health: June, September, December
Susceptible health areas: All Sense, Perception and Sensory Organs,
                                    Central Nervous System, Entire Body
                                    System related to "Leaks" and the
                                    Draining of Fluids, Feet and Toes,
                                    Insomnia, Respiratory System, Sometimes
                                    the Lungs and Intestines, Thyroid

MARCH 6   PISCES
Age for health changes: 6, 15, 24, 33, 42, 51, 60, 69, 78, 87
Months to guard health: May, October, November
Susceptible health areas: Entire Body System related to "Leaks" and
                                    the Draining of Fluids, Feet and Toes,
                                    Kidneys, Liver, Lumbar Region Disorders,
                                    Parathyroid, Sometimes the Lungs and
                                    Intestines, Throat, Veinous Circulation

MARCH 7   PISCES
Age for health changes: 7, 16, 25, 34, 43, 52, 61, 70, 79, 88

Months to guard health: January, February, July, August

Susceptible health areas: Depression from Mental Stress, Entire Body System related to "Leaks" and the Draining of Fluids, Feet and Toes, Prone to Drug or Alcohol Addiction, Sensitive Skin Conditions, Sometimes the Lungs and Intestines

MARCH 8   PISCES

Age for health changes: 8, 17, 26, 35, 44, 53, 62, 71, 80

Months to guard health: January, February, July, December

Susceptible health areas: Entire Body System related to "Leaks" and the Draining of Fluids, Feet and Toes, Gall Bladder, Headaches, Intestines, Liver Bile, Rheumatism, Skeletal System, Skin, Sometimes the Lungs, Spleen, Teeth

MARCH 9   PISCES

Age for health changes: 9, 18, 27, 36, 45, 54, 63, 72, 81

Months to guard health: April, May, October, November

Susceptible health areas: Chicken Pox, Contagious Diseases, Entire Body System related to "Leaks" and the Draining of Fluids, Feet and Toes, Kidneys, Measles, Muscular System, Red Corpuscles of the Blood, Sometimes the Lungs and Intestines

MARCH 10   PISCES

Age for health changes: 1, 10, 19, 28, 37, 46, 55, 64, 73, 82

Months to guard health: January, October, December

Susceptible health areas: Entire Body System related to "Leaks" and the Draining of Fluids, Eye Problems, Feet

and Toes, Headaches, Heart and
Circulatory System, High Blood Pressure,
Palpitations, Sometimes the Lungs and
Intestines

MARCH 11
Age for health changes:
Months to guard health:
Susceptible health areas:

PISCES
2, 11, 20, 29, 38, 47, 56, 65, 74, 83
January, February, July
Breasts, Digestive System Disorders,
Entire Body System related to "Leaks" and
the Draining of Fluids, Feet and Toes,
Lymphatic System Disorders, Ovaries,
Sometimes the Lungs and Intestines,
Stomach, Sympathetic Nervous System,
Synovial Fluids

MARCH 12
Age for health changes:
Months to guard health:
Susceptible health areas:

PISCES
3, 12, 21, 30, 39, 48, 57, 66, 75, 84
February, June, September, December
Entire Body System related to "Leaks" and
the Draining of Fluids, Excess Strain to
Nervous System, Feet and Toes, Liver,
Neuritis, Sciatica, Skin, Sometimes the
Lungs and Intestines, Throat

MARCH 13
Age for health changes:
Months to guard health:
Susceptible health areas:

PISCES
4, 13, 22, 31, 40, 49, 58, 67, 76, 85
January, February, July, August, September
Anemia, Back and Neck Pains, Cramps
and Spasms, Entire Body System related to
"Leaks" and the Draining of Fluids, Feet
and Toes, Melancholia, Mental Disorders,

Palpitations, Sometimes the Lungs and Intestines, Sudden Nervous Breakdowns

MARCH 14
Age for health changes:
Months to guard health:
Susceptible health areas:

PISCES
5, 14, 23, 32, 41, 50, 59, 68, 77, 86
June, September, December
All Sense, Perception and Sensory Organs, Central Nervous System, Entire Body System related to "Leaks" and the Draining of Fluids, Feet and Toes, Insomnia, Respiratory System, Sometimes the Lungs and Intestines, Thyroid

MARCH 15
Age for health changes:
Months to guard health:
Susceptible health areas:

PISCES
6, 15, 24, 33, 42, 51, 60, 69, 78, 87
May, October, November
Entire Body System related to "Leaks" and the Draining of Fluids, Feet and Toes, Kidneys, Liver, Lumbar Region Disorders, Parathyroid, Sometimes the Lungs and Intestines, Throat, Veinous Circulation

MARCH 16
Age for health changes:
Months to guard health:
Susceptible health areas:

PISCES
7, 16, 25, 34, 43, 52, 61, 70, 79, 88
January, February, July, August
Depression from Mental Stress, Entire Body System related to "Leaks" and the Draining of Fluids, Feet and Toes, Prone to Drug or Alcohol Addiction, Sensitive Skin Conditions, Sometimes the Lungs and Intestines

MARCH 17

Age for health changes: 8, 17, 26, 35, 44, 53, 62, 71, 80

Months to guard health: January, February, July, December

Susceptible health areas: Entire Body System related to "Leaks" and the Draining of Fluids, Feet and Toes, Gall Bladder, Headaches, Intestines, Liver Bile, Rheumatism, Skeletal System, Skin, Sometimes the Lungs, Spleen, Teeth

PISCES

MARCH 18

Age for health changes: 9, 18, 27, 36, 45, 54, 63, 72, 81

Months to guard health: April, May, October, November

Susceptible health areas: Chicken Pox, Contagious Diseases, Entire Body System related to "Leaks" and the Draining of Fluids, Feet and Toes, Kidneys, Measles, Muscular System, Red Corpuscles of the Blood, Sometimes the Lungs and Intestines

PISCES

MARCH 19

Age for health changes: 1, 10, 19, 28, 37, 46, 55, 64, 73, 82

Months to guard health: January, October, December

Susceptible health areas: Entire Body System related to "Leaks" and the Draining of Fluids, Eye Problems, Feet and Toes, Headaches, Heart and Circulatory System, High Blood Pressure, Palpitations, Sometimes the Lungs and Intestines

PISCES

MARCH 20

Age for health changes: 2, 11, 20, 29, 38, 47, 56, 65, 74, 83

Months to guard health: January, February, July

PISCES

Susceptible health areas: Breasts, Digestive System Disorders, Entire Body System related to "Leaks" and the Draining of Fluids, Feet and Toes, Lymphatic System Disorders, Ovaries, Sometimes the Lungs and Intestines, Stomach, Sympathetic Nervous System, Synovial Fluids

MARCH 21　　　　　　　ARIES
Age for health changes:　3, 12, 21, 30, 39, 48, 57, 66, 75, 84
Months to guard health:　February, June, September, December
Susceptible health areas:　Cerebral Hemisphere of the Brain, Excess Strain to Nervous System, Face (except nose), Head, Liver, Neuritis, Sciatica, Skin, Throat

MARCH 22　　　　　　　ARIES
Age for health changes:　4, 13, 22, 31, 40, 49, 58, 67, 76, 85
Months to guard health:　January, February, July, August, September
Susceptible health areas:　Anemia, Back and Neck Pains, Cerebral Hemisphere of the Brain, Cramps and Spasms, Face (except nose), Head, Melancholia, Mental Disorders, Palpitations, Sudden Nervous Breakdowns

MARCH 23　　　　　　　ARIES
Age for health changes:　5, 14, 23, 32, 41, 50, 59, 68, 77, 86
Months to guard health:　June, September, December
Susceptible health areas:　All Sense, Perception and Sensory Organs, Central Nervous System, Cerebral Hemisphere of the Brain, Face (except

nose), Head, Insomnia, Respiratory System, Thyroid

MARCH 24
Age for health changes:
Months to guard health:
Susceptible health areas:

ARIES
6, 15, 24, 33, 42, 51, 60, 69, 78, 87
May, October, November
Cerebral Hemisphere of the Brain, Face (except nose), Head, Kidneys, Liver, Lumbar Region Disorders, Parathyroid, Throat, Veinous Circulation

MARCH 25
Age for health changes:
Months to guard health:
Susceptible health areas:

ARIES
7, 16, 25, 34, 43, 52, 61, 70, 79, 88
January, February, July, August
Cerebral Hemisphere of the Brain, Depression from Mental Stress, Face (except nose), Head, Prone to Drug or Alcohol Addiction, Sensitive Skin Conditions

MARCH 26
Age for health changes:
Months to guard health:
Susceptible health areas:

ARIES
8, 17, 26, 35, 44, 53, 62, 71, 80
January, February, July, December
Cerebral Hemisphere of the Brain, Face (except nose), Gall Bladder, Head, Headaches, Intestines, Liver Bile, Rheumatism, Skeletal System, Skin, Spleen, Teeth

MARCH 27
Age for health changes:

ARIES
9, 18, 27, 36, 45, 54, 63, 72, 81

Months to guard health: April, May, October, November

Susceptible health areas: Cerebral Hemisphere of the Brain, Chicken Pox, Contagious Diseases, Face (except nose), Head, Kidneys, Measles, Muscular System, Red Corpuscles of the Blood

MARCH 28   ARIES

Age for health changes: 1, 10, 19, 28, 37, 46, 55, 64, 73, 82

Months to guard health: January, October, December

Susceptible health areas: Cerebral Hemisphere of the Brain, Eye Problems, Face (except nose), Head, Headaches, Heart and Circulatory System, High Blood Pressure, Palpitations

MARCH 29   ARIES

Age for health changes: 2, 11, 20, 29, 38, 47, 56, 65, 74, 83

Months to guard health: January, February, July

Susceptible health areas: Breasts, Cerebral Hemisphere of the Brain, Digestive System Disorders, Face (except nose), Head, Lymphatic System Disorders, Ovaries, Stomach, Sympathetic Nervous System, Synovial Fluids

MARCH 30   ARIES

Age for health changes: 3, 12, 21, 30, 39, 48, 57, 66, 75, 84

Months to guard health: February, June, September, December

Susceptible health areas: Cerebral Hemisphere of the Brain, Excess Strain to Nervous System, Face (except nose), Head, Liver, Neuritis, Sciatica, Skin, Throat

MARCH 31

Age for health changes:
Months to guard health:
Susceptible health areas:

ARIES

4, 13, 22, 31, 40, 49, 58, 67, 76, 85

January, February, July, August, September

Anemia, Back and Neck Pains, Cerebral Hemisphere of the Brain, Cramps and Spasms, Face (except nose), Head, Melancholia, Mental Disorders, Palpitations, Sudden Nervous Breakdowns

Health Cycles for April Birthdays

APRIL 1
Age for health changes:
Months to guard health:
Susceptible health areas:

ARIES
1, 10, 19, 28, 37, 46, 55, 64, 73, 82
January, October, December
Cerebral Hemisphere of the Brain, Eye Problems, Face (except nose), Head, Headaches, Heart and Circulatory System, High Blood Pressure, Palpitations

APRIL 2
Age for health changes:
Months to guard health:
Susceptible health areas:

ARIES
2, 11, 20, 29, 38, 47, 56, 65, 74, 83
January, February, July
Breasts, Cerebral Hemisphere of the Brain, Digestive System Disorders, Face (except nose), Head, Lymphatic System Disorders, Ovaries, Stomach, Sympathetic Nervous System, Synovial Fluids

APRIL 3
Age for health changes:
Months to guard health:
Susceptible health areas:

ARIES
3, 12, 21, 30, 39, 48, 57, 66, 75, 84
February, June, September, December
Cerebral Hemisphere of the Brain, Excess Strain to Nervous System, Face (except nose), Head, Liver, Neuritis, Sciatica, Skin, Throat

APRIL 4
Age for health changes:
Months to guard health:

ARIES
4, 13, 22, 31, 40, 49, 58, 67, 76, 85
January, February, July, August, September

Susceptible health areas: Anemia, Back and Neck Pains, Cerebral Hemisphere of the Brain, Cramps and Spasms, Face (except nose), Head, Melancholia, Mental Disorders, Palpitations, Sudden Nervous Breakdowns

APRIL 5 ARIES
Age for health changes: 5, 14, 23, 32, 41, 50, 59, 68, 77, 86
Months to guard health: June, September, December
Susceptible health areas: All Sense, Perception and Sensory Organs, Central Nervous System, Cerebral Hemisphere of the Brain, Face (except nose), Head, Insomnia, Respiratory System, Thyroid

APRIL 6 ARIES
Age for health changes: 6, 15, 24, 33, 42, 51, 60, 69, 78, 87
Months to guard health: May, October, November
Susceptible health areas: Cerebral Hemisphere of the Brain, Face (except nose), Head, Kidneys, Liver, Lumbar Region Disorders, Parathyroid, Throat, Veinous Circulation

APRIL 7 ARIES
Age for health changes: 7, 16, 25, 34, 43, 52, 61, 70, 79, 88
Months to guard health: January, February, July, August
Susceptible health areas: Cerebral Hemisphere of the Brain, Depression from Mental Stress, Face (except nose), Head, Prone to Drug or Alcohol Addiction, Sensitive Skin Conditions

APRIL 8
Age for health changes:
Months to guard health:
Susceptible health areas:

ARIES
8, 17, 26, 35, 44, 53, 62, 71, 80
January, February, July, December
Cerebral Hemisphere of the Brain, Face (except nose), Gall Bladder, Head, Headaches, Intestines, Liver Bile, Rheumatism, Skeletal System, Skin, Spleen, Teeth

APRIL 9
Age for health changes:
Months to guard health:
Susceptible health areas:

ARIES
9, 18, 27, 36, 45, 54, 63, 72, 81
April, May, October, November
Cerebral Hemisphere of the Brain, Chicken Pox, Contagious Diseases, Face (except nose), Head, Kidneys, Measles, Muscular System, Red Corpuscles of the Blood

APRIL 10
Age for health changes:
Months to guard health:
Susceptible health areas:

ARIES
1, 10, 19, 28, 37, 46, 55, 64, 73, 82
January, October, December
Cerebral Hemisphere of the Brain, Eye Problems, Face (except nose), Head, Headaches, Heart and Circulatory System, High Blood Pressure, Palpitations

APRIL 11
Age for health changes:
Months to guard health:
Susceptible health areas:

ARIES
2, 11, 20, 29, 38, 47, 56, 65, 74, 83
January, February, July
Breasts, Cerebral Hemisphere of the Brain, Digestive System Disorders, Face (except nose), Head, Lymphatic System Disorders,

Ovaries, Stomach, Sympathetic Nervous System, Synovial Fluids

APRIL 12   ARIES
Age for health changes: 3, 12, 21, 30, 39, 48, 57, 66, 75, 84
Months to guard health: February, June, September, December
Susceptible health areas: Cerebral Hemisphere of the Brain, Excess Strain to Nervous System, Face (except nose), Head, Liver, Neuritis, Sciatica, Skin, Throat

APRIL 13   ARIES
Age for health changes: 4, 13, 22, 31, 40, 49, 58, 67, 76, 85
Months to guard health: January, February, July, August, September
Susceptible health areas: Anemia, Back and Neck Pains, Cerebral Hemisphere of the Brain, Cramps and Spasms, Face (except nose), Head, Melancholia, Mental Disorders, Palpitations, Sudden Nervous Breakdowns

APRIL 14   ARIES
Age for health changes: 5, 14, 23, 32, 41, 50, 59, 68, 77, 86
Months to guard health: June, September, December
Susceptible health areas: All Sense, Perception and Sensory Organs, Central Nervous System, Cerebral Hemisphere of the Brain, Face (except nose), Head, Insomnia, Respiratory System, Thyroid

APRIL 15   ARIES
Age for health changes: 6, 15, 24, 33, 42, 51, 60, 69, 78, 87
Months to guard health: May, October, November

Susceptible health areas: Cerebral Hemisphere of the Brain, Face (except nose), Head, Kidneys, Liver, Lumbar Region Disorders, Parathyroid, Throat, Veinous Circulation

APRIL 16   ARIES
Age for health changes: 7, 16, 25, 34, 43, 52, 61, 70, 79, 88
Months to guard health: January, February, July, August
Susceptible health areas: Cerebral Hemisphere of the Brain, Depression from Mental Stress, Face (except nose), Head, Prone to Drug or Alcohol Addiction, Sensitive Skin Conditions

APRIL 17   ARIES
Age for health changes: 8, 17, 26, 35, 44, 53, 62, 71, 80
Months to guard health: January, February, July, December
Susceptible health areas: Cerebral Hemisphere of the Brain, Face (except nose), Gall Bladder, Head, Headaches, Intestines, Liver Bile, Rheumatism, Skeletal System, Skin, Spleen, Teeth

APRIL 18   ARIES
Age for health changes: 9, 18, 27, 36, 45, 54, 63, 72, 81
Months to guard health: April, May, October, November
Susceptible health areas: Cerebral Hemisphere of the Brain, Chicken Pox, Contagious Diseases, Face (except nose), Head, Kidneys, Measles, Muscular System, Red Corpuscles of the Blood

APRIL 19
Age for health changes:
Months to guard health:
Susceptible health areas:

ARIES
1, 10, 19, 28, 37, 46, 55, 64, 73, 82
January, October, December
Cerebral Hemisphere of the Brain, Eye Problems, Face (except nose), Head, Headaches, Heart and Circulatory System, High Blood Pressure, Palpitations

APRIL 20
Age for health changes:
Months to guard health:
Susceptible health areas:

TAURUS
2, 11, 20, 29, 38, 47, 56, 65, 74, 83
January, February, July
Breasts, Carotid Arteries, Digestive System Disorders, Jugular Vein, Larynx, Lymphatic System Disorders, Neck, Ovaries, Stomach, Sympathetic Nervous System, Synovial Fluids, Throat, Tonsils

APRIL 21
Age for health changes:
Months to guard health:
Susceptible health areas:

TAURUS
3, 12, 21, 30, 39, 48, 57, 66, 75, 84
February, June, September, December
Carotid Arteries, Excess Strain to Nervous System, Jugular Vein, Larynx, Liver, Neck, Neuritis, Sciatica, Skin, Throat, Tonsils

APRIL 22
Age for health changes:
Months to guard health:
Susceptible health areas:

TAURUS
4, 13, 22, 31, 40, 49, 58, 67, 76, 85
January, February, July, August, September
Anemia, Back and Neck Pains, Carotid Arteries, Cramps and Spasms, Jugular Vein, Larynx, Neck, Melancholia, Mental Disorders, Palpitations, Sudden Nervous Breakdowns, Throat, Tonsils

APRIL 23
Age for health changes:
Months to guard health:
Susceptible health areas:

TAURUS
5, 14, 23, 32, 41, 50, 59, 68, 77, 86
June, September, December
All Sense, Perception and Sensory Organs, Carotid Arteries, Central Nervous System, Insomnia, Jugular Vein, Larynx, Neck, Respiratory System, Throat, Thyroid, Tonsils

APRIL 24
Age for health changes:
Months to guard health:
Susceptible health areas:

TAURIS
6, 15, 24, 33, 42, 51, 60, 69, 78, 87
May, October, November
Carotid Arteries, Jugular Vein, Larynx, Kidneys, Liver, Lumbar Region Disorders, Neck, Parathyroid, Throat, Tonsils, Veinous Circulation

APRIL 25
Age for health changes:
Months to guard health:
Susceptible health areas:

TAURUS
7, 16, 25, 34, 43, 52, 61, 70, 79, 88
January, February, July, August
Carotid Arteries, Depression from Mental Stress, Jugular Vein, Larynx, Neck, Prone to Drug or Alcohol Addiction, Sensitive Skin Conditions, Throat, Tonsils

APRIL 26
Age for health changes:
Months to guard health:
Susceptible health areas:

TAURUS
8, 17, 26, 35, 44, 53, 62, 71, 80
January, February, July, December
Carotid Arteries, Gall Bladder, Headaches, Intestines, Jugular Vein, Larynx, Liver

Bile, Neck, Rheumatism, Skeletal System, Skin, Spleen, Teeth, Throat, Tonsils

APRIL 27   TAURUS
Age for health changes: 9, 18, 27, 36, 45, 54, 63, 72, 81
Months to guard health: April, May, October, November
Susceptible health areas: Carotid   Arteries,   Chicken   Pox,
                                Contagious   Diseases,   Jugular   Vein,
                                Kidneys,   Larynx,   Measles,   Muscular
                                System,   Neck,   Red   Corpuscles   of   the
                                Blood, Throat, Tonsils

APRIL 28   TAURUS
Age for health changes: 1, 10, 19, 28, 37, 46, 55, 64, 73, 82
Months to guard health: January, October, December
Susceptible health areas: Carotid   Arteries,   Eye   Problems,
                                Headaches, Heart and Circulatory System,
                                High   Blood   Pressure,   Jugular   Vein,
                                Larynx,   Neck,   Palpitations,   Throat,
                                Tonsils

APRIL 29   TAURUS
Age for health changes: 2, 11, 20, 29, 38, 47, 56, 65, 74, 83
Months to guard health: January, February, July
Susceptible health areas: Breasts, Carotid Arteries, Digestive System
                                Disorders,   Jugular   Vein,   Larynx,
                                Lymphatic   System   Disorders,   Neck,
                                Ovaries, Stomach, Sympathetic Nervous
                                System, Synovial Fluids, Throat, Tonsils

APRIL 30   TAURUS
Age for health changes: 3, 12, 21, 30, 39, 48, 57, 66, 75, 84

| Months to guard health: | February, June, September, December |
| Susceptible health areas: | Carotid Arteries, Excess Strain to Nervous System, Jugular Vein, Larynx, Liver, Neck, Neuritis, Sciatica, Skin, Throat, Tonsils |

Health Cycles for May Birthdays

MAY 1

Age for health changes:
Months to guard health:
Susceptible health areas:

TAURUS

1, 10, 19, 28, 37, 46, 55, 64, 73, 82

January, October, December

Carotid Arteries, Eye Problems, Headaches, Heart and Circulatory System, High Blood Pressure, Jugular Vein, Larynx, Neck, Palpitations, Throat, Tonsils

MAY 2

Age for health changes:
Months to guard health:
Susceptible health areas:

TAURUS

2, 11, 20, 29, 38, 47, 56, 65, 74, 83

January, February, July

Breasts, Carotid Arteries, Digestive System Disorders, Jugular Vein, Larynx, Lymphatic System Disorders, Neck, Ovaries, Stomach, Sympathetic Nervous System, Synovial Fluids, Throat, Tonsils

MAY 3

Age for health changes:
Months to guard health:
Susceptible health areas:

TAURUS

3, 12, 21, 30, 39, 48, 57, 66, 75, 84

February, June, September, December

Carotid Arteries, Excess Strain to Nervous System, Jugular Vein, Larynx, Liver, Neck, Neuritis, Sciatica, Skin, Throat, Tonsils

MAY 4

Age for health changes:
Months to guard health:

TAURUS

4, 13, 22, 31, 40, 49, 58, 67, 76, 85

January, February, July, August, September

Susceptible health areas:	Anemia, Back and Neck Pains, Carotid Arteries, Cramps and Spasms, Jugular Vein, Larynx, Neck, Melancholia, Mental Disorders, Palpitations, Sudden Nervous Breakdowns, Throat, Tonsils

MAY 5 TAURUS
Age for health changes: 5, 14, 23, 32, 41, 50, 59, 68, 77, 86
Months to guard health: June, September, December
Susceptible health areas: All Sense, Perception and Sensory Organs, Carotid Arteries, Central Nervous System, Insomnia, Jugular Vein, Larynx, Neck, Respiratory System, Throat, Thyroid, Tonsils

MAY 6 TAURIS
Age for health changes: 6, 15, 24, 33, 42, 51, 60, 69, 78, 87
Months to guard health: May, October, November
Susceptible health areas: Carotid Arteries, Jugular Vein, Larynx, Kidneys, Liver, Lumbar Region Disorders, Neck, Parathyroid, Throat, Tonsils, Veinous Circulation

MAY 7 TAURUS
Age for health changes: 7, 16, 25, 34, 43, 52, 61, 70, 79, 88
Months to guard health: January, February, July, August
Susceptible health areas: Carotid Arteries, Depression from Mental Stress, Jugular Vein, Larynx, Neck, Prone to Drug or Alcohol Addiction, Sensitive Skin Conditions, Throat, Tonsils

MAY 8

Age for health changes:
Months to guard health:
Susceptible health areas:

TAURUS

8, 17, 26, 35, 44, 53, 62, 71, 80
January, February, July, December
Carotid Arteries, Gall Bladder, Headaches, Intestines, Jugular Vein, Larynx, Liver Bile, Neck, Rheumatism, Skeletal System, Skin, Spleen, Teeth, Throat, Tonsils

MAY 9

Age for health changes:
Months to guard health:
Susceptible health areas:

TAURUS

9, 18, 27, 36, 45, 54, 63, 72, 81
April, May, October, November
Carotid Arteries, Chicken Pox, Contagious Diseases, Jugular Vein, Kidneys, Larynx, Measles, Muscular System, Neck, Red Corpuscles of the Blood, Throat, Tonsils

MAY 10

Age for health changes:
Months to guard health:
Susceptible health areas:

TAURUS

1, 10, 19, 28, 37, 46, 55, 64, 73, 82
January, October, December
Carotid Arteries, Eye Problems, Headaches, Heart and Circulatory System, High Blood Pressure, Jugular Vein, Larynx, Neck, Palpitations, Throat, Tonsils

MAY 11

Age for health changes:
Months to guard health:
Susceptible health areas:

TAURUS

2, 11, 20, 29, 38, 47, 56, 65, 74, 83
January, February, July
Breasts, Carotid Arteries, Digestive System Disorders, Jugular Vein, Larynx, Lymphatic System Disorders, Neck,

Ovaries, Stomach, Sympathetic Nervous System, Synovial Fluids, Throat, Tonsils

MAY 12   TAURUS
Age for health changes: 3, 12, 21, 30, 39, 48, 57, 66, 75, 84
Months to guard health: February, June, September, December
Susceptible health areas: Carotid Arteries, Excess Strain to Nervous System, Jugular Vein, Larynx, Liver, Neck, Neuritis, Sciatica, Skin, Throat, Tonsils

MAY 13   TAURUS
Age for health changes: 4, 13, 22, 31, 40, 49, 58, 67, 76, 85
Months to guard health: January, February, July, August, September
Susceptible health areas: Anemia, Back and Neck Pains, Carotid Arteries, Cramps and Spasms, Jugular Vein, Larynx, Neck, Melancholia, Mental Disorders, Palpitations, Sudden Nervous Breakdowns, Throat, Tonsils

MAY 14   TAURUS
Age for health changes: 5, 14, 23, 32, 41, 50, 59, 68, 77, 86
Months to guard health: June, September, December
Susceptible health areas: All Sense, Perception and Sensory Organs, Carotid Arteries, Central Nervous System, Insomnia, Jugular Vein, Larynx, Neck, Respiratory System, Throat, Thyroid, Tonsils

MAY 15   TAURIS
Age for health changes: 6, 15, 24, 33, 42, 51, 60, 69, 78, 87
Months to guard health: May, October, November

Susceptible health areas: Carotid Arteries, Jugular Vein, Larynx, Kidneys, Liver, Lumbar Region Disorders, Neck, Parathyroid, Throat, Tonsils, Veinous Circulation

MAY 16   TAURUS
Age for health changes: 7, 16, 25, 34, 43, 52, 61, 70, 79, 88
Months to guard health: January, February, July, August
Susceptible health areas: Carotid Arteries, Depression from Mental Stress, Jugular Vein, Larynx, Neck, Prone to Drug or Alcohol Addiction, Sensitive Skin Conditions, Throat, Tonsils

MAY 17   TAURUS
Age for health changes: 8, 17, 26, 35, 44, 53, 62, 71, 80
Months to guard health: January, February, July, December
Susceptible health areas: Carotid Arteries, Gall Bladder, Headaches, Intestines, Jugular Vein, Larynx, Liver Bile, Neck, Rheumatism, Skeletal System, Skin, Spleen, Teeth, Throat, Tonsils

MAY 18   TAURUS
Age for health changes: 9, 18, 27, 36, 45, 54, 63, 72, 81
Months to guard health: April, May, October, November
Susceptible health areas: Carotid Arteries, Chicken Pox, Contagious Diseases, Jugular Vein, Kidneys, Larynx, Measles, Muscular System, Neck, Red Corpuscles of the Blood, Throat, Tonsils

MAY 19   TAURUS
Age for health changes: 1, 10, 19, 28, 37, 46, 55, 64, 73, 82

Months to guard health: January, October, December
Susceptible health areas: Carotid Arteries, Eye Problems, Headaches, Heart and Circulatory System, High Blood Pressure, Jugular Vein, Larynx, Neck, Palpitations, Throat, Tonsils

MAY 20 TAURUS
Age for health changes: 2, 11, 20, 29, 38, 47, 56, 65, 74, 83
Months to guard health: January, February, July
Susceptible health areas: Breasts, Carotid Arteries, Digestive System Disorders, Jugular Vein, Larynx, Lymphatic System Disorders, Neck, Ovaries, Stomach, Sympathetic Nervous System, Synovial Fluids, Throat, Tonsils

MAY 21 GEMINI
Age for health changes: 3, 12, 21, 30, 39, 48, 57, 66, 75, 84
Months to guard health: February, June, September, December
Susceptible health areas: Arms, Excess Strain to Nervous System, Fingers, Hands, Liver, Lungs, Nerves, Neuritis, Sciatica, Shoulders, Skin, Throat, Thymus, Upper Ribs

MAY 22 GEMINI
Age for health changes: 4, 13, 22, 31, 40, 49, 58, 67, 76, 85
Months to guard health: January, February, July, August, September
Susceptible health areas: Anemia, Arms, Back and Neck Pains, Cramps and Spasms, Fingers, Hands, Lungs, Melancholia, Mental Disorders, Nerves, Palpitations, Shoulders, Sudden Nervous Breakdowns, Thymus, Upper Ribs

MAY 23
Age for health changes:
Months to guard health:
Susceptible health areas:

GEMINI
5, 14, 23, 32, 41, 50, 59, 68, 77, 86
June, September, December
All Sense, Perception and Sensory Organs, Arms, Central Nervous System, Fingers, Hands, Insomnia, Lungs, Nerves, Respiratory System, Shoulders, Thyroid, Thymus, Upper Ribs

MAY 24
Age for health changes:
Months to guard health:
Susceptible health areas:

GEMINI
6, 15, 24, 33, 42, 51, 60, 69, 78, 87
May, October, November
Arms, Fingers, Hands, Kidneys, Liver, Lumbar Region Disorders, Lungs, Nerves, Parathyroid, Shoulders, Throat, Thymus, Upper Ribs, Veinous Circulation

MAY 25
Age for health changes:
Months to guard health:
Susceptible health areas:

GEMINI
7, 16, 25, 34, 43, 52, 61, 70, 79, 88
January, February, July, August
Arms, Depression from Mental Stress, Fingers, Hands, Lungs, Nerves, Prone to Drug or Alcohol Addiction, Sensitive Skin Conditions, Shoulders, Thymus, Upper Ribs

MAY 26
Age for health changes:
Months to guard health:
Susceptible health areas:

GEMINI
8, 17, 26, 35, 44, 53, 62, 71, 80
January, February, July, December
Arms, Fingers, Hands, Gall Bladder, Headaches, Intestines, Liver Bile, Lungs,

Nerves, Rheumatism, Shoulders, Skeletal System, Skin, Spleen, Teeth, Thymus, Upper Ribs

MAY 27
Age for health changes:
Months to guard health:
Susceptible health areas:

GEMINI
9, 18, 27, 36, 45, 54, 63, 72, 81
April, May, October, November
Arms, Chicken Pox, Contagious Diseases, Fingers, Hands, Kidneys, Lungs, Measles, Muscular System, Nerves, Red Corpuscles of the Blood, Shoulders, Thymus, Upper Ribs

MAY 28
Age for health changes:
Months to guard health:
Susceptible health areas:

GEMINI
1, 10, 19, 28, 37, 46, 55, 64, 73, 82
January, October, December
Arms, Eye Problems, Fingers, Hands, Headaches, Heart and Circulatory System, High Blood Pressure, Lungs, Nerves, Palpitations, Shoulders, Thymus, Upper Ribs

MAY 29
Age for health changes:
Months to guard health:
Susceptible health areas:

GEMINI
2, 11, 20, 29, 38, 47, 56, 65, 74, 83
January, February, July
Arms, Breasts, Digestive System Disorders, Fingers, Hands, Lungs, Lymphatic System Disorders, Nerves, Ovaries, Shoulders, Stomach, Sympathetic Nervous System, Synovial Fluids, Thymus, Upper Ribs

MAY 30
Age for health changes:
Months to guard health:
Susceptible health areas:

GEMINI
3, 12, 21, 30, 39, 48, 57, 66, 75, 84
February, June, September, December
Arms, Excess Strain to Nervous System, Fingers, Hands, Liver, Lungs, Nerves, Neuritis, Sciatica, Shoulders, Skin, Throat, Thymus, Upper Ribs

MAY 31
Age for health changes:
Months to guard health:
Susceptible health areas:

GEMINI
4, 13, 22, 31, 40, 49, 58, 67, 76, 85
January, February, July, August, September
Anemia, Arms, Back and Neck Pains, Cramps and Spasms, Fingers, Hands, Lungs, Melancholia, Mental Disorders, Nerves, Palpitations, Shoulders, Sudden Nervous Breakdowns, Thymus, Upper Ribs

Health Cycles for June Birthdays

JUNE 1
Age for health changes:
Months to guard health:
Susceptible health areas:

GEMINI
1, 10, 19, 28, 37, 46, 55, 64, 73, 82
January, October, December
Arms, Eye Problems, Fingers, Hands, Headaches, Heart and Circulatory System, High Blood Pressure, Lungs, Nerves, Palpitations, Shoulders, Thymus, Upper Ribs

JUNE 2
Age for health changes:
Months to guard health:
Susceptible health areas:

GEMINI
2, 11, 20, 29, 38, 47, 56, 65, 74, 83
January, February, July
Arms, Breasts, Digestive System Disorders, Fingers, Hands, Lungs, Lymphatic System Disorders, Nerves, Ovaries, Shoulders, Stomach, Sympathetic Nervous System, Synovial Fluids, Thymus, Upper Ribs

JUNE 3
Age for health changes:
Months to guard health:
Susceptible health areas:

GEMINI
3, 12, 21, 30, 39, 48, 57, 66, 75, 84
February, June, September, December
Arms, Excess Strain to Nervous System, Fingers, Hands, Liver, Lungs, Nerves, Neuritis, Sciatica, Shoulders, Skin, Throat, Thymus, Upper Ribs

JUNE 4
Age for health changes:

GEMINI
4, 13, 22, 31, 40, 49, 58, 67, 76, 85

Months to guard health: January, February, July, August, September
Susceptible health areas: Anemia, Arms, Back and Neck Pains, Cramps and Spasms, Fingers, Hands, Lungs, Melancholia, Mental Disorders, Nerves, Palpitations, Shoulders, Sudden Nervous Breakdowns, Thymus, Upper Ribs

JUNE 5 GEMINI
Age for health changes: 5, 14, 23, 32, 41, 50, 59, 68, 77, 86
Months to guard health: June, September, December
Susceptible health areas: All Sense, Perception and Sensory Organs, Arms, Central Nervous System, Fingers, Hands, Insomnia, Lungs, Nerves, Respiratory System, Shoulders, Thyroid, Thymus, Upper Ribs

JUNE 6 GEMINI
Age for health changes: 6, 15, 24, 33, 42, 51, 60, 69, 78, 87
Months to guard health: June, October, November
Susceptible health areas: Arms, Fingers, Hands, Kidneys, Liver, Lumbar Region Disorders, Lungs, Nerves, Parathyroid, Shoulders, Throat, Thymus, Upper Ribs, Veinous Circulation

JUNE 7 GEMINI
Age for health changes: 7, 16, 25, 34, 43, 52, 61, 70, 79, 88
Months to guard health: January, February, July, August
Susceptible health areas: Arms, Depression from Mental Stress, Fingers, Hands, Lungs, Nerves, Prone to Drug or Alcohol Addiction, Sensitive Skin

Conditions, Shoulders, Thymus, Upper Ribs

JUNE 8
Age for health changes:
Months to guard health:
Susceptible health areas:

GEMINI
8, 17, 26, 35, 44, 53, 62, 71, 80
January, February, July, December
Arms, Fingers, Hands, Gall Bladder, Headaches, Intestines, Liver Bile, Lungs, Nerves, Rheumatism, Shoulders, Skeletal System, Skin, Spleen, Teeth, Thymus, Upper Ribs

JUNE 9
Age for health changes:
Months to guard health:
Susceptible health areas:

GEMINI
9, 18, 27, 36, 45, 54, 63, 72, 81
April, June, October, November
Arms, Chicken Pox, Contagious Diseases, Fingers, Hands, Kidneys, Lungs, Measles, Muscular System, Nerves, Red Corpuscles of the Blood, Shoulders, Thymus, Upper Ribs

JUNE 10
Age for health changes:
Months to guard health:
Susceptible health areas:

GEMINI
1, 10, 19, 28, 37, 46, 55, 64, 73, 82
January, October, December
Arms, Eye Problems, Fingers, Hands, Headaches, Heart and Circulatory System, High Blood Pressure, Lungs, Nerves, Palpitations, Shoulders, Thymus, Upper Ribs

JUNE 11
Age for health changes:

GEMINI
2, 11, 20, 29, 38, 47, 56, 65, 74, 83

Months to guard health: January, February, July
Susceptible health areas: Arms, Breasts, Digestive System Disorders, Fingers, Hands, Lungs, Lymphatic System Disorders, Nerves, Ovaries, Shoulders, Stomach, Sympathetic Nervous System, Synovial Fluids, Thymus, Upper Ribs

JUNE 12 GEMINI
Age for health changes: 3, 12, 21, 30, 39, 48, 57, 66, 75, 84
Months to guard health: February, June, September, December
Susceptible health areas: Arms, Excess Strain to Nervous System, Fingers, Hands, Liver, Lungs, Nerves, Neuritis, Sciatica, Shoulders, Skin, Throat, Thymus, Upper Ribs

JUNE 13 GEMINI
Age for health changes: 4, 13, 22, 31, 40, 49, 58, 67, 76, 85
Months to guard health: January, February, July, August, September
Susceptible health areas: Anemia, Arms, Back and Neck Pains, Cramps and Spasms, Fingers, Hands, Lungs, Melancholia, Mental Disorders, Nerves, Palpitations, Shoulders, Sudden Nervous Breakdowns, Thymus, Upper Ribs

JUNE 14 GEMINI
Age for health changes: 5, 14, 23, 32, 41, 50, 59, 68, 77, 86
Months to guard health: June, September, December
Susceptible health areas: All Sense, Perception and Sensory Organs, Arms, Central Nervous System, Fingers, Hands, Insomnia, Lungs, Nerves,

Respiratory System, Shoulders, Thyroid, Thymus, Upper Ribs

JUNE 15

Age for health changes:
Months to guard health:
Susceptible health areas:

GEMINI
6, 15, 24, 33, 42, 51, 60, 69, 78, 87
June, October, November
Arms, Fingers, Hands, Kidneys, Liver, Lumbar Region Disorders, Lungs, Nerves, Parathyroid, Shoulders, Throat, Thymus, Upper Ribs, Veinous Circulation

JUNE 16

Age for health changes:
Months to guard health:
Susceptible health areas:

GEMINI
7, 16, 25, 34, 43, 52, 61, 70, 79, 88
January, February, July, August
Arms, Depression from Mental Stress, Fingers, Hands, Lungs, Nerves, Prone to Drug or Alcohol Addiction, Sensitive Skin Conditions, Shoulders, Thymus, Upper Ribs

JUNE 17

Age for health changes:
Months to guard health:
Susceptible health areas:

GEMINI
8, 17, 26, 35, 44, 53, 62, 71, 80
January, February, July, December
Arms, Fingers, Hands, Gall Bladder, Headaches, Intestines, Liver Bile, Lungs, Nerves, Rheumatism, Shoulders, Skeletal System, Skin, Spleen, Teeth, Thymus, Upper Ribs

JUNE 18

Age for health changes:
Months to guard health:

GEMINI
9, 18, 27, 36, 45, 54, 63, 72, 81
April, June, October, November

Susceptible health areas: Arms, Chicken Pox, Contagious Diseases, Fingers, Hands, Kidneys, Lungs, Measles, Muscular System, Nerves, Red Corpuscles of the Blood, Shoulders, Thymus, Upper Ribs

JUNE 19   GEMINI
Age for health changes: 1, 10, 19, 28, 37, 46, 55, 64, 73, 82
Months to guard health: January, October, December
Susceptible health areas: Arms, Eye Problems, Fingers, Hands, Headaches, Heart and Circulatory System, High Blood Pressure, Lungs, Nerves, Palpitations, Shoulders, Thymus, Upper Ribs

JUNE 20   GEMINI
Age for health changes: 2, 11, 20, 29, 38, 47, 56, 65, 74, 83
Months to guard health: January, February, July
Susceptible health areas: Arms, Breasts, Digestive System Disorders, Fingers, Hands, Lungs, Lymphatic System Disorders, Nerves, Ovaries, Shoulders, Stomach, Sympathetic Nervous System, Synovial Fluids, Thymus, Upper Ribs

JUNE 21   GEMINI
Age for health changes: 3, 12, 21, 30, 39, 48, 57, 66, 75, 84
Months to guard health: February, June, September, December
Susceptible health areas: Arms, Excess Strain to Nervous System, Fingers, Hands, Liver, Lungs, Nerves, Neuritis, Sciatica, Shoulders, Skin, Throat, Thymus, Upper Ribs

JUNE 22
Age for health changes:
Months to guard health:
Susceptible health areas:

CANCER
4, 13, 22, 31, 40, 49, 58, 67, 76, 85
January, February, July, August, September
Anemia, Back and Neck Pains, Breasts, Chest, Cramps and Spasms, Diaphragm, Lymph System, Melancholia, Mental Disorders, Palpitations, Sudden Nervous Breakdowns, Thoracic Duct

JUNE 23
Age for health changes:
Months to guard health:
Susceptible health areas:

CANCER
5, 14, 23, 32, 41, 50, 59, 68, 77, 86
June, September, December
All Sense, Perception and Sensory Organs; Breasts, Central Nervous System, Chest, Diaphragm, Insomnia, Lymph System, Thoracic Duct, Thyroid

JUNE 24
Age for health changes:
Months to guard health:
Susceptible health areas:

CANCER
6, 15, 24, 33, 42, 51, 60, 69, 78, 87
June, October, November
Breasts, Chest, Diaphragm, Kidneys, Liver, Lumbar Region Disorders, Lymph System, Parathyroid, Stomach, Thoracic Duct, Throat, Veinous Circulation

JUNE 25
Age for health changes:
Months to guard health:
Susceptible health areas:

CANCER
7, 16, 25, 34, 43, 52, 61, 70, 79, 88
January, February, July, August
Breasts, Chest, Depression Caused by Mental Stress, Diaphragm, Lymph System, Prone to Drug or Alcohol

Addiction, Sensitive Skin Conditions, Thoracic Duct

JUNE 26
Age for health changes:
Months to guard health:
Susceptible health areas:

CANCER
8, 17, 26, 35, 44, 53, 62, 71, 80
January, February, July, December
Breasts, Chest, Diaphragm, Gall Bladder, Headaches, Intestines, Liver Bile, Lymph System, Rheumatism, Skeletal System, Skin, Spleen, Teeth, Thoracic Duct

JUNE 27
Age for health changes:
Months to guard health:
Susceptible health areas:

CANCER
9, 18, 27, 36, 45, 54, 63, 72, 81
April, June, October, November
Breasts, Chest, Chicken Pox, Contagious Diseases, Diaphragm, Kidneys, Lymph System, Measles, Muscular System, Red Corpuscles of the Blood, Thoracic Duct

JUNE 28
Age for health changes:
Months to guard health:
Susceptible health areas:

CANCER
1, 10, 19, 28, 37, 46, 55, 64, 73, 82
January, October, December
Breasts, Chest, Diaphragm, Eye Problems, Headaches, Heart and Circulatory System, High Blood Pressure, Lymph System, Palpitations, Thoracic Duct

JUNE 29
Age for health changes:
Months to guard health:
Susceptible health areas:

CANCER
2, 11, 20, 29, 38, 47, 56, 65, 74, 83
January, February, July
Breasts, Chest, Diaphragm, Digestive System Disorders, Lymphatic System

Disorders, Ovaries, Stomach, Sympathetic Nervous System, Synovial Fluids, Thoracic Duct

JUNE 30

Age for health changes:
Months to guard health:
Susceptible health areas:

CANCER

3, 12, 21, 30, 39, 48, 57, 66, 75, 84

February, June, September, December

Breasts, Chest, Diaphragm, Excess Strain to Nervous System, Liver, Lymph System, Neuritis, Sciatica, Skin, Thoracic Duct, Throat

Health Cycles for July Birthdays

JULY 1
Age for health changes:
Months to guard health:
Susceptible health areas:

CANCER
1, 10, 19, 28, 37, 46, 55, 64, 73, 82
January, October, December
Breasts, Chest, Diaphragm, Eye Problems, Headaches, Heart and Circulatory System, High Blood Pressure, Lymph System, Palpitations, Thoracic Duct

JULY 2
Age for health changes:
Months to guard health:
Susceptible health areas:

CANCER
2, 11, 20, 29, 38, 47, 56, 65, 74, 83
January, February, July
Breasts, Chest, Diaphragm, Digestive System Disorders, Lymphatic System Disorders, Ovaries, Stomach, Sympathetic Nervous System, Synovial Fluids, Thoracic Duct

JULY 3
Age for health changes:
Months to guard health:
Susceptible health areas:

CANCER
3, 12, 21, 30, 39, 48, 57, 66, 75, 84
February, June, September, December
Breasts, Chest, Diaphragm, Excess Strain to Nervous System, Liver, Lymph System, Neuritis, Sciatica, Skin, Thoracic Duct, Throat

JULY 4
Age for health changes:
Months to guard health:

CANCER
4, 13, 22, 31, 40, 49, 58, 67, 76, 85
January, February, July, August, September

Susceptible health areas:	Anemia, Back and Neck Pains, Breasts, Chest, Cramps and Spasms, Diaphragm, Lymph System, Melancholia, Mental Disorders, Palpitations, Sudden Nervous Breakdowns, Thoracic Duct

JULY 5 — CANCER
Age for health changes: 5, 14, 23, 32, 41, 50, 59, 68, 77, 86
Months to guard health: June, September, December
Susceptible health areas: All Sense, Perception and Sensory Organs; Breasts, Central Nervous System, Chest, Diaphragm, Insomnia, Lymph System, Thoracic Duct, Thyroid

JULY 6 — CANCER
Age for health changes: 6, 15, 24, 33, 42, 51, 60, 69, 78, 87
Months to guard health: June, October, November
Susceptible health areas: Breasts, Chest, Diaphragm, Kidneys, Liver, Lumbar Region Disorders, Lymph System, Parathyroid, Stomach, Thoracic Duct, Throat, Veinous Circulation

JULY 7 — CANCER
Age for health changes: 7, 16, 25, 34, 43, 52, 61, 70, 79, 88
Months to guard health: January, February, July, August
Susceptible health areas: Breasts, Chest, Depression Caused by Mental Stress, Diaphragm, Lymph System, Prone to Drug or Alcohol Addiction, Sensitive Skin Conditions, Thoracic Duct

JULY 8
Age for health changes:
Months to guard health:
Susceptible health areas:

CANCER
8, 17, 26, 35, 44, 53, 62, 71, 80
January, February, July, December
Breasts, Chest, Diaphragm, Gall Bladder, Headaches, Intestines, Liver Bile, Lymph System, Rheumatism, Skeletal System, Skin, Spleen, Teeth, Thoracic Duct

JULY 9
Age for health changes:
Months to guard health:
Susceptible health areas:

CANCER
9, 18, 27, 36, 45, 54, 63, 72, 81
April, June, October, November
Breasts, Chest, Chicken Pox, Contagious Diseases, Diaphragm, Kidneys, Lymph System, Measles, Muscular System, Red Corpuscles of the Blood, Thoracic Duct

JULY 10
Age for health changes:
Months to guard health:
Susceptible health areas:

CANCER
1, 10, 19, 28, 37, 46, 55, 64, 73, 82
January, October, December
Breasts, Chest, Diaphragm, Eye Problems, Headaches, Heart and Circulatory System, High Blood Pressure, Lymph System, Palpitations, Thoracic Duct

JULY 11
Age for health changes:
Months to guard health:
Susceptible health areas:

CANCER
2, 11, 20, 29, 38, 47, 56, 65, 74, 83
January, February, July
Breasts, Chest, Diaphragm, Digestive System Disorders, Lymphatic System Disorders, Ovaries, Stomach, Sympathetic Nervous System, Synovial Fluids, Thoracic Duct

JULY 12   CANCER
Age for health changes: 3, 12, 21, 30, 39, 48, 57, 66, 75, 84
Months to guard health: February, June, September, December
Susceptible health areas: Breasts, Chest, Diaphragm, Excess Strain
                                    to Nervous System, Liver, Lymph System,
                                    Neuritis, Sciatica, Skin, Thoracic Duct,
                                    Throat

JULY 13   CANCER
Age for health changes: 4, 13, 22, 31, 40, 49, 58, 67, 76, 85
Months to guard health: January, February, July, August, September
Susceptible health areas: Anemia, Back and Neck Pains, Breasts,
                                    Chest, Cramps and Spasms, Diaphragm,
                                    Lymph System, Melancholia, Mental
                                    Disorders, Palpitations, Sudden Nervous
                                    Breakdowns, Thoracic Duct

JULY 14   CANCER
Age for health changes: 5, 14, 23, 32, 41, 50, 59, 68, 77, 86
Months to guard health: June, September, December
Susceptible health areas: All Sense, Perception and Sensory Organs;
                                    Breasts, Central Nervous System, Chest,
                                    Diaphragm, Insomnia, Lymph System,
                                    Thoracic Duct, Thyroid

JULY 15   CANCER
Age for health changes: 6, 15, 24, 33, 42, 51, 60, 69, 78, 87
Months to guard health: June, October, November
Susceptible health areas: Breasts, Chest, Diaphragm, Kidneys,
                                    Liver, Lumbar Region Disorders, Lymph

System, Parathyroid, Stomach, Thoracic Duct, Throat, Veinous Circulation

JULY 16

Age for health changes:
Months to guard health:
Susceptible health areas:

CANCER

7, 16, 25, 34, 43, 52, 61, 70, 79, 88
January, February, July, August
Breasts, Chest, Depression Caused by Mental Stress, Diaphragm, Lymph System, Prone to Drug or Alcohol Addiction, Sensitive Skin Conditions, Thoracic Duct

JULY 17

Age for health changes:
Months to guard health:
Susceptible health areas:

CANCER

8, 17, 26, 35, 44, 53, 62, 71, 80
January, February, July, December
Breasts, Chest, Diaphragm, Gall Bladder, Headaches, Intestines, Liver Bile, Lymph System, Rheumatism, Skeletal System, Skin, Spleen, Teeth, Thoracic Duct

JULY 18

Age for health changes:
Months to guard health:
Susceptible health areas:

CANCER

9, 18, 27, 36, 45, 54, 63, 72, 81
April, June, October, November
Breasts, Chest, Chicken Pox, Contagious Diseases, Diaphragm, Kidneys, Lymph System, Measles, Muscular System, Red Corpuscles of the Blood, Thoracic Duct

JULY 19

Age for health changes:
Months to guard health:

CANCER

1, 10, 19, 28, 37, 46, 55, 64, 73, 82
January, October, December

Susceptible health areas:	Breasts, Chest, Diaphragm, Eye Problems, Headaches, Heart and Circulatory System, High Blood Pressure, Lymph System, Palpitations, Thoracic Duct

JULY 20   CANCER
Age for health changes: 2, 11, 20, 29, 38, 47, 56, 65, 74, 83
Months to guard health: January, February, July
Susceptible health areas: Breasts, Chest, Diaphragm, Digestive System Disorders, Lymphatic System Disorders, Ovaries, Stomach, Sympathetic Nervous System, Synovial Fluids, Thoracic Duct

JULY 21   CANCER
Age for health changes: 3, 12, 21, 30, 39, 48, 57, 66, 75, 84
Months to guard health: February, June, September, December
Susceptible health areas: Breasts, Chest, Diaphragm, Excess Strain to Nervous System, Liver, Lymph System, Neuritis, Sciatica, Skin, Thoracic Duct, Throat

JULY 22   CANCER
Age for health changes: 4, 13, 22, 31, 40, 49, 58, 67, 76, 85
Months to guard health: January, February, July, August, September
Susceptible health areas: Anemia, Back and Neck Pains, Breasts, Chest, Cramps and Spasms, Diaphragm, Lymph System, Melancholia, Mental Disorders, Palpitations, Sudden Nervous Breakdowns, Thoracic Duct

JULY 23
Age for health changes:
Months to guard health:
Susceptible health areas:

LEO
5, 14, 23, 32, 41, 50, 59, 68, 77, 86
June, September, December
All Sense, Perception and Sensory Organs, Aorta, Back, Central Nervous System, Heart, Insomnia, Respiratory System, Spinal Cord, Thyroid

JULY 24
Age for health changes:
Months to guard health:
Susceptible health areas:

LEO
6, 15, 24, 33, 42, 51, 60, 69, 78, 87
June, October, November
Aorta, Back, Heart, Kidneys, Liver, Lumbar Region Disorders, Parathyroid, Spinal Cord, Throat

JULY 25
Age for health changes:
Months to guard health:
Susceptible health areas:

LEO
7, 16, 25, 34, 43, 52, 61, 70, 79, 88
January, February, July, August
Aorta, Back, Depression Caused by Mental Stress, Heart, Prone to Drug or Alcohol Addiction, Sensitive Skin Conditions, Spinal Cord

JULY 26
Age for health changes:
Months to guard health:
Susceptible health areas:

LEO
8, 17, 26, 35, 44, 53, 62, 71, 80
January, February, July, December
Aorta, Back, Gall Bladder, Headaches, Heart, Intestines, Liver Bile, Rheumatism, Skeletal System, Skin, Spinal Cord, Spleen, Teeth

JULY 27
Age for health changes:
Months to guard health:
Susceptible health areas:

LEO
9, 18, 27, 36, 45, 54, 63, 72, 81
April, June, October, November
Aorta, Back, Chicken Pox, Contagious Diseases, Heart, Kidneys, Measles, Muscular System, Red Corpuscles of the Blood, Spinal Cord

JULY 28
Age for health changes:
Months to guard health:
Susceptible health areas:

LEO
1, 10, 19, 28, 37, 46, 55, 64, 73, 82
January, October, December
Aorta, Back, Eye Problems, Headaches, Heart and Circulatory System, High Blood Pressure, Palpitations, Spinal Cord

JULY 29
Age for health changes:
Months to guard health:
Susceptible health areas:

LEO
2, 11, 20, 29, 38, 47, 56, 65, 74, 83
January, February, July
Aorta, Back, Breasts, Digestive System Disorders, Heart, Lymphatic System Disorders, Ovaries, Spinal Cord, Stomach, Sympathetic Nervous System, Synovial Fluids

JULY 30
Age for health changes:
Months to guard health:
Susceptible health areas:

LEO
3, 12, 21, 30, 39, 48, 57, 66, 75, 84
February, June, September, December
Aorta, Back, Excess Strain to Nervous System, Heart, Liver, Neuritis, Sciatica, Skin, Spinal Cord, Throat

JULY 31
Age for health changes:
Months to guard health:
Susceptible health areas:

LEO
4, 13, 22, 31, 40, 49, 58, 67, 76, 85
January, February, July, August, September
Anemia, Aorta, Back and Neck Pains, Cramps and Spasms, Heart, Melancholia, Mental Disorders, Palpitations, Spinal Cord, Sudden Nervous Breakdowns

Health Cycles for August Birthdays

AUGUST 1
Age for health changes:
Months to guard health:
Susceptible health areas:

LEO
1, 10, 19, 28, 37, 46, 55, 64, 73, 82
January, October, December
Aorta, Back, Eye Problems, Headaches, Heart and Circulatory System, High Blood Pressure, Palpitations, Spinal Cord

AUGUST 2
Age for health changes:
Months to guard health:
Susceptible health areas:

LEO
2, 11, 20, 29, 38, 47, 56, 65, 74, 83
January, February, July
Aorta, Back, Breasts, Digestive System Disorders, Heart, Lymphatic System Disorders, Ovaries, Spinal Cord, Stomach, Sympathetic Nervous System, Synovial Fluids

AUGUST 3
Age for health changes:
Months to guard health:
Susceptible health areas:

LEO
3, 12, 21, 30, 39, 48, 57, 66, 75, 84
February, June, September, December
Aorta, Back, Excess Strain to Nervous System, Heart, Liver, Neuritis, Sciatica, Skin, Spinal Cord, Throat

AUGUST 4
Age for health changes:
Months to guard health:
Susceptible health areas:

LEO
4, 13, 22, 31, 40, 49, 58, 67, 76, 85
January, February, July, August, September
Anemia, Aorta, Back and Neck Pains, Cramps and Spasms, Heart, Melancholia,

Mental Disorders, Palpitations, Spinal Cord, Sudden Nervous Breakdowns

AUGUST 5
Age for health changes:
Months to guard health:
Susceptible health areas:

LEO
5, 14, 23, 32, 41, 50, 59, 68, 77, 86
June, September, December
All Sense, Perception and Sensory Organs, Aorta, Back, Central Nervous System, Heart, Insomnia, Respiratory System, Spinal Cord, Thyroid

AUGUST 6
Age for health changes:
Months to guard health:
Susceptible health areas:

LEO
6, 15, 24, 33, 42, 51, 60, 69, 78, 87
June, October, November
Aorta, Back, Heart, Kidneys, Liver, Lumbar Region Disorders, Parathyroid, Spinal Cord, Throat

AUGUST 7
Age for health changes:
Months to guard health:
Susceptible health areas:

LEO
7, 16, 25, 34, 43, 52, 61, 70, 79, 88
January, February, July, August
Aorta, Back, Depression Caused by Mental Stress, Heart, Prone to Drug or Alcohol Addiction, Sensitive Skin Conditions, Spinal Cord

AUGUST 8
Age for health changes:
Months to guard health:
Susceptible health areas:

LEO
8, 17, 26, 35, 44, 53, 62, 71, 80
January, February, July, December
Aorta, Back, Gall Bladder, Headaches, Heart, Intestines, Liver Bile, Rheumatism,

Skeletal System, Skin, Spinal Cord, Spleen, Teeth

AUGUST 9 — LEO
Age for health changes: 9, 18, 27, 36, 45, 54, 63, 72, 81
Months to guard health: April, June, October, November
Susceptible health areas: Aorta, Back, Chicken Pox, Contagious Diseases, Heart, Kidneys, Measles, Muscular System, Red Corpuscles of the Blood, Spinal Cord

AUGUST 10 — LEO
Age for health changes: 1, 10, 19, 28, 37, 46, 55, 64, 73, 82
Months to guard health: January, October, December
Susceptible health areas: Aorta, Back, Eye Problems, Headaches, Heart and Circulatory System, High Blood Pressure, Palpitations, Spinal Cord

AUGUST 11 — LEO
Age for health changes: 2, 11, 20, 29, 38, 47, 56, 65, 74, 83
Months to guard health: January, February, July
Susceptible health areas: Aorta, Back, Breasts, Digestive System Disorders, Heart, Lymphatic System Disorders, Ovaries, Spinal Cord, Stomach, Sympathetic Nervous System, Synovial Fluids

AUGUST 12 — LEO
Age for health changes: 3, 12, 21, 30, 39, 48, 57, 66, 75, 84
Months to guard health: February, June, September, December

Susceptible health areas: Aorta, Back, Excess Strain to Nervous System, Heart, Liver, Neuritis, Sciatica, Skin, Spinal Cord, Throat

AUGUST 13 LEO
Age for health changes: 4, 13, 22, 31, 40, 49, 58, 67, 76, 85
Months to guard health: January, February, July, August, September
Susceptible health areas: Anemia, Aorta, Back and Neck Pains, Cramps and Spasms, Heart, Melancholia, Mental Disorders, Palpitations, Spinal Cord, Sudden Nervous Breakdowns

AUGUST 14 LEO
Age for health changes: 5, 14, 23, 32, 41, 50, 59, 68, 77, 86
Months to guard health: June, September, December
Susceptible health areas: All Sense, Perception and Sensory Organs, Aorta, Back, Central Nervous System, Heart, Insomnia, Respiratory System, Spinal Cord, Thyroid

AUGUST 15 LEO
Age for health changes: 6, 15, 24, 33, 42, 51, 60, 69, 78, 87
Months to guard health: June, October, November
Susceptible health areas: Aorta, Back, Heart, Kidneys, Liver, Lumbar Region Disorders, Parathyroid, Spinal Cord, Throat

AUGUST 16 LEO
Age for health changes: 7, 16, 25, 34, 43, 52, 61, 70, 79, 88
Months to guard health: January, February, July, August
Susceptible health areas: Aorta, Back, Depression Caused by Mental Stress, Heart, Prone to Drug or

Alcohol Addiction, Sensitive Skin Conditions, Spinal Cord

AUGUST 17
Age for health changes:
Months to guard health:
Susceptible health areas:

LEO
8, 17, 26, 35, 44, 53, 62, 71, 80
January, February, July, December
Aorta, Back, Gall Bladder, Headaches, Heart, Intestines, Liver Bile, Rheumatism, Skeletal System, Skin, Spinal Cord, Spleen, Teeth

AUGUST 18
Age for health changes:
Months to guard health:
Susceptible health areas:

LEO
9, 18, 27, 36, 45, 54, 63, 72, 81
April, June, October, November
Aorta, Back, Chicken Pox, Contagious Diseases, Heart, Kidneys, Measles, Muscular System, Red Corpuscles of the Blood, Spinal Cord

AUGUST 19
Age for health changes:
Months to guard health:
Susceptible health areas:

LEO
1, 10, 19, 28, 37, 46, 55, 64, 73, 82
January, October, December
Aorta, Back, Eye Problems, Headaches, Heart and Circulatory System, High Blood Pressure, Palpitations, Spinal Cord

AUGUST 20
Age for health changes:
Months to guard health:
Susceptible health areas:

LEO
2, 11, 20, 29, 38, 47, 56, 65, 74, 83
January, February, July
Aorta, Back, Breasts, Digestive System Disorders, Heart, Lymphatic System Disorders, Ovaries, Spinal Cord, Stomach,

Sympathetic Nervous System, Synovial Fluids

AUGUST 21
Age for health changes:
Months to guard health:
Susceptible health areas:

LEO
3, 12, 21, 30, 39, 48, 57, 66, 75, 84
February, June, September, December
Aorta, Back, Excess Strain to Nervous System, Heart, Liver, Neuritis, Sciatica, Skin, Spinal Cord, Throat

AUGUST 22
Age for health changes:
Months to guard health:
Susceptible health areas:

LEO
4, 13, 22, 31, 40, 49, 58, 67, 76, 85
January, February, July, August, September
Anemia, Aorta, Back and Neck Pains, Cramps and Spasms, Heart, Melancholia, Mental Disorders, Palpitations, Spinal Cord, Sudden Nervous Breakdowns

AUGUST 23
Age for health changes:
Months to guard health:
Susceptible health areas:

VIRGO
5, 14, 23, 32, 41, 50, 59, 68, 77, 86
June, September, December
All Sense, Perception and Sensory Organs, Central Nervous System, Insomnia, Large and Small Intestines, Nervous System, Pancreas, Respiratory System, Thyroid

AUGUST 24
Age for health changes:
Months to guard health:
Susceptible health areas:

VIRGO
6, 15, 24, 33, 42, 51, 60, 69, 78, 87
June, October, November
Large and Small Intestines, Kidneys, Liver, Lumbar Region Disorders, Nervous

System, Pancreas, Parathyroid, Throat, Veinous Circulation

AUGUST 25
Age for health changes:
Months to guard health:
Susceptible health areas:

VIRGO
7, 16, 25, 34, 43, 52, 61, 70, 79, 88
January, February, July, August
Depression Caused by Mental Stress, Large and Small Intestines, Nervous System, Pancreas, Prone to Drug or Alcohol Addiction, Sensitive Skin conditions

AUGUST 26
Age for health changes:
Months to guard health:
Susceptible health areas:

VIRGO
8, 17, 26, 35, 44, 53, 62, 71, 80
January, February, July, December
Gall Bladder, Headaches, Large and Small Intestines, Liver Bile, Nervous System, Pancreas, Skeletal System, Skin, Spleen, Rheumatism, Teeth

AUGUST 27
Age for health changes:
Months to guard health:
Susceptible health areas:

VIRGO
9, 18, 27, 36, 45, 54, 63, 72, 81
April, June, October, November
Chicken Pox, Contagious Diseases, Kidneys, Large and Small Intestines, Measles, Muscular System, Nervous System, Pancreas, Red Corpuscles of the Blood

AUGUST 28
Age for health changes:
Months to guard health:

VIRGO
1, 10, 19, 28, 37, 46, 55, 64, 73, 82
January, October, December

| Susceptible health areas: | Eye Problems, Headaches, Heart and Circulatory System, High Blood Pressure, Large and Small Intestines, Nervous System, Palpitations, Pancreas |

AUGUST 29
Age for health changes:
Months to guard health:
Susceptible health areas:

VIRGO
2, 11, 20, 29, 38, 47, 56, 65, 74, 83
January, February, July
Breasts, Digestive System Disorders, Large and Small Intestines, Lymphatic System Disorders, Nervous System, Ovaries, Pancreas, Stomach, Sympathetic Nervous System, Synovial Fluids

AUGUST 30
Age for health changes:
Months to guard health:
Susceptible health areas:

VIRGO
3, 12, 21, 30, 39, 48, 57, 66, 75, 84
February, June, September, December
Excess Strain to Nervous System, Large and Small Intestines, Liver, Nervous System, Neuritis, Pancreas, Sciatica, Skin, Throat

AUGUST 31
Age for health changes:
Months to guard health:
Susceptible health areas:

VIRGO
4, 13, 22, 31, 40, 49, 58, 67, 76, 85
January, February, July, August, September
Anemia, Back and Neck Pains, Cramps and Spasms, Large and Small Intestines, Melancholia, Mental Disorders, Nervous System, Palpitations, Pancreas, Sudden Nervous Breakdowns

Health Cycles for September Birthdays

SEPTEMBER 1
Age for health changes:
Months to guard health:
Susceptible health areas:

VIRGO
1, 10, 19, 28, 37, 46, 55, 64, 73, 82
January, October, December
Eye Problems, Headaches, Heart and Circulatory System, High Blood Pressure, Large and Small Intestines, Nervous System, Palpitations, Pancreas

SEPTEMBER 2
Age for health changes:
Months to guard health:
Susceptible health areas:

VIRGO
2, 11, 20, 29, 38, 47, 56, 65, 74, 83
January, February, July
Breasts, Digestive System Disorders, Large and Small Intestines, Lymphatic System Disorders, Nervous System, Ovaries, Pancreas, Stomach, Sympathetic Nervous System, Synovial Fluids

SEPTEMBER 3
Age for health changes:
Months to guard health:
Susceptible health areas:

VIRGO
3, 12, 21, 30, 39, 48, 57, 66, 75, 84
February, June, September, December
Excess Strain to Nervous System, Large and Small Intestines, Liver, Nervous System, Neuritis, Pancreas, Sciatica, Skin, Throat

SEPTEMBER 4
Age for health changes:
Months to guard health:

VIRGO
4, 13, 22, 31, 40, 49, 58, 67, 76, 85
January, February, July, August, September

179

Susceptible health areas:	Anemia, Back and Neck Pains, Cramps and Spasms, Large and Small Intestines, Melancholia, Mental Disorders, Nervous System, Palpitations, Pancreas, Sudden Nervous Breakdowns

SEPTEMBER 5 — VIRGO

Age for health changes:	5, 14, 23, 32, 41, 50, 59, 68, 77, 86
Months to guard health:	June, September, December
Susceptible health areas:	All Sense, Perception and Sensory Organs, Central Nervous System, Insomnia, Large and Small Intestines, Nervous System, Pancreas, Respiratory System, Thyroid

SEPTEMBER 6 — VIRGO

Age for health changes:	6, 15, 24, 33, 42, 51, 60, 69, 78, 87
Months to guard health:	June, October, November
Susceptible health areas:	Large and Small Intestines, Kidneys, Liver, Lumbar Region Disorders, Nervous System, Pancreas, Parathyroid, Throat, Veinous Circulation

SEPTEMBER 7 — VIRGO

Age for health changes:	7, 16, 25, 34, 43, 52, 61, 70, 79, 88
Months to guard health:	January, February, July, August
Susceptible health areas:	Depression Caused by Mental Stress, Large and Small Intestines, Nervous System, Pancreas, Prone to Drug or Alcohol Addiction, Sensitive Skin conditions

SEPTEMBER 8 — VIRGO

Age for health changes:	8, 17, 26, 35, 44, 53, 62, 71, 80

Months to guard health:	January, February, July, December
Susceptible health areas:	Gall Bladder, Headaches, Large and Small Intestines, Liver Bile, Nervous System, Pancreas, Skeletal System, Skin, Spleen, Rheumatism, Teeth

SEPTEMBER 9 — VIRGO

Age for health changes:	9, 18, 27, 36, 45, 54, 63, 72, 81
Months to guard health:	April, June, October, November
Susceptible health areas:	Chicken Pox, Contagious Diseases, Kidneys, Large and Small Intestines, Measles, Muscular System, Nervous System, Pancreas, Red Corpuscles of the Blood

SEPTEMBER 10 — VIRGO

Age for health changes:	1, 10, 19, 28, 37, 46, 55, 64, 73, 82
Months to guard health:	January, October, December
Susceptible health areas:	Eye Problems, Headaches, Heart and Circulatory System, High Blood Pressure, Large and Small Intestines, Nervous System, Palpitations, Pancreas

SEPTEMBER 11 — VIRGO

Age for health changes:	2, 11, 20, 29, 38, 47, 56, 65, 74, 83
Months to guard health:	January, February, July
Susceptible health areas:	Breasts, Digestive System Disorders, Large and Small Intestines, Lymphatic System Disorders, Nervous System, Ovaries, Pancreas, Stomach, Sympathetic Nervous System, Synovial Fluids

SEPTEMBER 12
Age for health changes:
Months to guard health:
Susceptible health areas:

VIRGO
3, 12, 21, 30, 39, 48, 57, 66, 75, 84
February, June, September, December
Excess Strain to Nervous System, Large and Small Intestines, Liver, Nervous System, Neuritis, Pancreas, Sciatica, Skin, Throat

SEPTEMBER 13
Age for health changes:
Months to guard health:
Susceptible health areas:

VIRGO
4, 13, 22, 31, 40, 49, 58, 67, 76, 85
January, February, July, August, September
Anemia, Back and Neck Pains, Cramps and Spasms, Large and Small Intestines, Melancholia, Mental Disorders, Nervous System, Palpitations, Pancreas, Sudden Nervous Breakdowns

SEPTEMBER 14
Age for health changes:
Months to guard health:
Susceptible health areas:

VIRGO
5, 14, 23, 32, 41, 50, 59, 68, 77, 86
June, September, December
All Sense, Perception and Sensory Organs, Central Nervous System, Insomnia, Large and Small Intestines, Nervous System, Pancreas, Respiratory System, Thyroid

SEPTEMBER 15
Age for health changes:
Months to guard health:
Susceptible health areas:

VIRGO
6, 15, 24, 33, 42, 51, 60, 69, 78, 87
June, October, November
Large and Small Intestines, Kidneys, Liver, Lumbar Region Disorders, Nervous System, Pancreas, Parathyroid, Throat, Veinous Circulation

SEPTEMBER 16
Age for health changes:
Months to guard health:
Susceptible health areas:

VIRGO
7, 16, 25, 34, 43, 52, 61, 70, 79, 88
January, February, July, August
Depression Caused by Mental Stress, Large and Small Intestines, Nervous System, Pancreas, Prone to Drug or Alcohol Addiction, Sensitive Skin conditions

SEPTEMBER 17
Age for health changes:
Months to guard health:
Susceptible health areas:

VIRGO
8, 17, 26, 35, 44, 53, 62, 71, 80
January, February, July, December
Gall Bladder, Headaches, Large and Small Intestines, Liver Bile, Nervous System, Pancreas, Skeletal System, Skin, Spleen, Rheumatism, Teeth

SEPTEMBER 18
Age for health changes:
Months to guard health:
Susceptible health areas:

VIRGO
9, 18, 27, 36, 45, 54, 63, 72, 81
April, June, October, November
Chicken Pox, Contagious Diseases, Kidneys, Large and Small Intestines, Measles, Muscular System, Nervous System, Pancreas, Red Corpuscles of the Blood

SEPTEMBER 19
Age for health changes:
Months to guard health:
Susceptible health areas:

VIRGO
1, 10, 19, 28, 37, 46, 55, 64, 73, 82
January, October, December
Eye Problems, Headaches, Heart and Circulatory System, High Blood Pressure,

Large and Small Intestines, Nervous System, Palpitations, Pancreas

SEPTEMBER 20
Age for health changes:
Months to guard health:
Susceptible health areas:

VIRGO
2, 11, 20, 29, 38, 47, 56, 65, 74, 83
January, February, July
Breasts, Digestive System Disorders, Large and Small Intestines, Lymphatic System Disorders, Nervous System, Ovaries, Pancreas, Stomach, Sympathetic Nervous System, Synovial Fluids

SEPTEMBER 21
Age for health changes:
Months to guard health:
Susceptible health areas:

VIRGO
3, 12, 21, 30, 39, 48, 57, 66, 75, 84
February, June, September, December
Excess Strain to Nervous System, Large and Small Intestines, Liver, Nervous System, Neuritis, Pancreas, Sciatica, Skin, Throat

SEPTEMBER 22
Age for health changes:
Months to guard health:
Susceptible health areas:

VIRGO
4, 13, 22, 31, 40, 49, 58, 67, 76, 85
January, February, July, August, September
Anemia, Back and Neck Pains, Cramps and Spasms, Large and Small Intestines, Melancholia, Mental Disorders, Nervous System, Palpitations, Pancreas, Sudden Nervous Breakdowns

SEPTEMBER 23
Age for health changes:
Months to guard health:

LIBRA
5, 14, 23, 32, 41, 50, 59, 68, 77, 86
June, September, December

| Susceptible health areas: | All Sense, Perception and Sensory Organs, Central Nervous System, Equilibrium and Balance, Insomnia, Kidneys, Respiratory System, Sometimes the Skin, Thyroid |

SEPTEMBER 24 LIBRA
Age for health changes: 6, 15, 24, 33, 42, 51, 60, 69, 78, 87
Months to guard health: June, October, November
Susceptible health areas: Equilibrium and Balance, Kidneys, Liver, Lumbar Region Disorders, Parathyroid, Sometimes the Skin, Throat, Veinous Circulation

SEPTEMBER 25 LIBRA
Age for health changes: 7, 16, 25, 34, 43, 52, 61, 70, 79, 88
Months to guard health: January, February, July, August
Susceptible health areas: Depression Caused by Mental Stress, Equilibrium and Balance, Kidneys, Prone to Drug and Alcohol Addiction, Sensitive Skin Conditions

SEPTEMBER 26 LIBRA
Age for health changes: 8, 17, 26, 35, 44, 53, 62, 71, 80
Months to guard health: January, February, July, December
Susceptible health areas: Equilibrium and Balance, Headaches, Gall Bladder, Kidneys, Liver Bile, Intestines, Rheumatism, Skeletal System, Skin, Spleen, Teeth

SEPTEMBER 27 LIBRA
Age for health changes: 9, 18, 27, 36, 45, 54, 63, 72, 81
Months to guard health: April, June, October, November

Susceptible health areas:	Chicken Pox, Contagious Diseases, Equilibrium and Balance, Kidneys, Measles, Muscular System, Red Corpuscles of the Blood, Sometimes the Skin

SEPTEMBER 28

	LIBRA
Age for health changes:	1, 10, 19, 28, 37, 46, 55, 64, 73, 82
Months to guard health:	January, October, December
Susceptible health areas:	Equilibrium and Balance, Eye Problems, Heart and Circulatory System, Headaches, High Blood Pressure, Kidneys, Palpitations, Sometimes the Skin

SEPTEMBER 29

	LIBRA
Age for health changes:	2, 11, 20, 29, 38, 47, 56, 65, 74, 83
Months to guard health:	January, February, July
Susceptible health areas:	Breasts, Digestive System Disorders, Equilibrium and Balance, Kidneys, Lymphatic System Disorders, Ovaries, Sometimes the Skin, Stomach, Sympathetic Nervous System, Synovial Fluids

SEPTEMBER 30

	LIBRA
Age for health changes:	3, 12, 21, 30, 39, 48, 57, 66, 75, 84
Months to guard health:	February, June, September, December
Susceptible health areas:	Equilibrium and Balance, Excess Strain to Nervous System, Kidneys, Liver, Neuritis, Sciatica, Skin, Throat

Health Cycles for October Birthdays

OCTOBER 1
Age for health changes:
Months to guard health:
Susceptible health areas:

LIBRA
1, 10, 19, 28, 37, 46, 55, 64, 73, 82
January, October, December
Equilibrium and Balance, Eye Problems,
Heart and Circulatory System, Headaches,
High Blood Pressure, Kidneys,
Palpitations, Sometimes the Skin

OCTOBER 2
Age for health changes:
Months to guard health:
Susceptible health areas:

LIBRA
2, 11, 20, 29, 38, 47, 56, 65, 74, 83
January, February, July
Breasts, Digestive System Disorders,
Equilibrium and Balance, Kidneys,
Lymphatic System Disorders, Ovaries,
Sometimes the Skin, Stomach,
Sympathetic Nervous System, Synovial
Fluids

OCTOBER 3
Age for health changes:
Months to guard health:
Susceptible health areas:

LIBRA
3, 12, 21, 30, 39, 48, 57, 66, 75, 84
February, June, September, December
Equilibrium and Balance, Excess Strain to
Nervous System, Kidneys, Liver, Neuritis,
Sciatica, Skin, Throat

OCTOBER 4
Age for health changes:
Months to guard health:

LIBRA
4, 13, 22, 31, 40, 49, 58, 67, 76, 85
January, February, July, August, September

Susceptible health areas: Equilibrium and Balance, Excess Strain to Nervous System, Kidneys, Liver, Neuritis, Sciatica, Skin, Throat

OCTOBER 5   LIBRA
Age for health changes: 5, 14, 23, 32, 41, 50, 59, 68, 77, 86
Months to guard health: June, September, December
Susceptible health areas: All Sense, Perception and Sensory Organs, Central Nervous System, Equilibrium and Balance, Insomnia, Kidneys, Respiratory System, Sometimes the Skin, Thyroid

OCTOBER 6   LIBRA
Age for health changes: 6, 15, 24, 33, 42, 51, 60, 69, 78, 87
Months to guard health: June, October, November
Susceptible health areas: Equilibrium and Balance, Kidneys, Liver, Lumbar Region Disorders, Parathyroid, Sometimes the Skin, Throat, Veinous Circulation

OCTOBER 7   LIBRA
Age for health changes: 7, 16, 25, 34, 43, 52, 61, 70, 79, 88
Months to guard health: January, February, July, August
Susceptible health areas: Depression Caused by Mental Stress, Equilibrium and Balance, Kidneys, Prone to Drug and Alcohol Addiction, Sensitive Skin Conditions

OCTOBER 8   LIBRA
Age for health changes: 8, 17, 26, 35, 44, 53, 62, 71, 80
Months to guard health: January, February, July, December

Susceptible health areas:	Equilibrium and Balance, Headaches, Gall Bladder, Kidneys, Liver Bile, Intestines, Rheumatism, Skeletal System, Skin, Spleen, Teeth

OCTOBER 9

LIBRA

Age for health changes: 9, 18, 27, 36, 45, 54, 63, 72, 81

Months to guard health: April, June, October, November

Susceptible health areas: Chicken Pox, Contagious Diseases, Equilibrium and Balance, Kidneys, Measles, Muscular System, Red Corpuscles of the Blood, Sometimes the Skin

OCTOBER 10

LIBRA

Age for health changes: 1, 10, 19, 28, 37, 46, 55, 64, 73, 82

Months to guard health: January, October, December

Susceptible health areas: Equilibrium and Balance, Eye Problems, Heart and Circulatory System, Headaches, High Blood Pressure, Kidneys, Palpitations, Sometimes the Skin

OCTOBER 11

LIBRA

Age for health changes: 2, 11, 20, 29, 38, 47, 56, 65, 74, 83

Months to guard health: January, February, July

Susceptible health areas: Breasts, Digestive System Disorders, Equilibrium and Balance, Kidneys, Lymphatic System Disorders, Ovaries, Sometimes the Skin, Stomach, Sympathetic Nervous System, Synovial Fluids

OCTOBER 12

Age for health changes:
Months to guard health:
Susceptible health areas:

LIBRA

3, 12, 21, 30, 39, 48, 57, 66, 75, 84
February, June, September, December
Equilibrium and Balance, Excess Strain to
Nervous System, Kidneys, Liver, Neuritis,
Sciatica, Skin, Throat

OCTOBER 13

Age for health changes:
Months to guard health:
Susceptible health areas:

LIBRA

4, 13, 22, 31, 40, 49, 58, 67, 76, 85
January, February, July, August, September
Equilibrium and Balance, Excess Strain to
Nervous System, Kidneys, Liver, Neuritis,
Sciatica, Skin, Throat

OCTOBER 14

Age for health changes:
Months to guard health:
Susceptible health areas:

LIBRA

5, 14, 23, 32, 41, 50, 59, 68, 77, 86
June, September, December
All Sense, Perception and Sensory Organs,
Central Nervous System, Equilibrium and
Balance, Insomnia, Kidneys, Respiratory
System, Sometimes the Skin, Thyroid

OCTOBER 15

Age for health changes:
Months to guard health:
Susceptible health areas:

LIBRA

6, 15, 24, 33, 42, 51, 60, 69, 78, 87
June, October, November
Equilibrium and Balance, Kidneys, Liver,
Lumbar Region Disorders, Parathyroid,
Sometimes the Skin, Throat, Veinous
Circulation

OCTOBER 16

Age for health changes:

LIBRA

7, 16, 25, 34, 43, 52, 61, 70, 79, 88

| Months to guard health: | January, February, July, August |
| Susceptible health areas: | Depression Caused by Mental Stress, Equilibrium and Balance, Kidneys, Prone to Drug and Alcohol Addiction, Sensitive Skin Conditions |

OCTOBER 17   LIBRA
Age for health changes: 8, 17, 26, 35, 44, 53, 62, 71, 80
Months to guard health: January, February, July, December
Susceptible health areas: Equilibrium and Balance, Headaches, Gall Bladder, Kidneys, Liver Bile, Intestines, Rheumatism, Skeletal System, Skin, Spleen, Teeth

OCTOBER 18   LIBRA
Age for health changes: 9, 18, 27, 36, 45, 54, 63, 72, 81
Months to guard health: April, June, October, November
Susceptible health areas: Chicken Pox, Contagious Diseases, Equilibrium and Balance, Kidneys, Measles, Muscular System, Red Corpuscles of the Blood, Sometimes the Skin

OCTOBER 19   LIBRA
Age for health changes: 1, 10, 19, 28, 37, 46, 55, 64, 73, 82
Months to guard health: January, October, December
Susceptible health areas: Equilibrium and Balance, Eye Problems, Heart and Circulatory System, Headaches, High Blood Pressure, Kidneys, Palpitations, Sometimes the Skin

OCTOBER 20
Age for health changes:
Months to guard health:
Susceptible health areas:

LIBRA
2, 11, 20, 29, 38, 47, 56, 65, 74, 83
January, February, July
Breasts, Digestive System Disorders, Equilibrium and Balance, Kidneys, Lymphatic System Disorders, Ovaries, Sometimes the Skin, Stomach, Sympathetic Nervous System, Synovial Fluids

OCTOBER 21
Age for health changes:
Months to guard health:
Susceptible health areas:

LIBRA
3, 12, 21, 30, 39, 48, 57, 66, 75, 84
February, June, September, December
Equilibrium and Balance, Excess Strain to Nervous System, Kidneys, Liver, Neuritis, Sciatica, Skin, Throat

OCTOBER 22
Age for health changes:
Months to guard health:
Susceptible health areas:

LIBRA
4, 13, 22, 31, 40, 49, 58, 67, 76, 85
January, February, July, August, September
Equilibrium and Balance, Excess Strain to Nervous System, Kidneys, Liver, Neuritis, Sciatica, Skin, Throat

OCTOBER 23
Age for health changes:
Months to guard health:
Susceptible health areas:

SCORPIO
5, 14, 23, 32, 41, 50, 59, 68, 77, 86
June, September, December
All Sense, Perception and Sensory Organs, the Blood, Central Nervous System, Descending Colon, Genitals, Insomnia, Nose, Rectum, Reproductive Organs,

Respiratory System, Sometimes the Back, Thyroid, Urethra

OCTOBER 24   SCORPIO
Age for health changes: 6, 15, 24, 33, 42, 51, 60, 69, 78, 87
Months to guard health: June, October, November
Susceptible health areas: The Blood, Descending Colon, Genitals, Kidneys, Liver, Lumbar Region Disorders, Nose, Parathyroid, Rectum, Reproductive Organs, Sometimes the Back, Throat, Urethra, Veinous Circulation

OCTOBER 25   SCORPIO
Age for health changes: 7, 16, 25, 34, 43, 52, 61, 70, 79, 88
Months to guard health: January, February, July, August
Susceptible health areas: The Blood, Depression Caused by Mental Stress, Descending Colon, Genitals, Nose, Prone to Drug and Alcohol or Addiction, Rectum, Reproductive Organs, Sensitive Skin Conditions, Sometimes the Back, Urethra

OCTOBER 26   SCORPIO
Age for health changes: 8, 17, 26, 35, 44, 53, 62, 71, 80, 89
Months to guard health: January, February, July, December
Susceptible health areas: The Blood, Descending Colon, Headaches, Gall Bladder, Genitals, Intestines, Liver Bile, Nose, Rectum, Reproductive Organs, Rheumatism, Skeletal system, Skin, Spleen, Sometimes the Back, Teeth, Urethra

OCTOBER 27
Age for health changes:
Months to guard health:
Susceptible health areas:

SCORPIO
9, 18, 27, 36, 45, 54, 63, 72, 81
April, June, October, November
Contagious Diseases, Chicken Pox, Descending Colon, Genitals, Kidneys, Measles, Muscular System, Nose, Rectum, Red Corpuscles of the Blood, Reproductive Organs, Sometimes the Back, Urethra

OCTOBER 28
Age for health changes:
Months to guard health:
Susceptible health areas:

SCORPIO
1, 10, 19, 28, 37, 46, 55, 64, 73, 82
January, October, December
The Blood, Descending Colon, Eye Problems, Genitals, Headaches, Heart and Circulatory System, High Blood Pressure, Nose, Palpitations, Rectum, Reproductive Organs, Sometimes the Back, Urethra

OCTOBER 29
Age for health changes:
Months to guard health:
Susceptible health areas:

SCORPIO
2, 11, 20, 29, 38, 47, 56, 65, 74, 83
January, February, July
The Blood, Breasts, Descending Colon, Digestive System Disorders, Genitals, Lymphatic System Disorders, Nose, Ovaries, Rectum, Reproductive Organs, Sometimes the Back, Stomach, Sympathetic Nervous System, Synovial Fluids, Urethra

OCTOBER 30
Age for health changes:

SCORPIO
3, 12, 21, 30, 39, 48, 57, 66, 75, 84

Months to guard health: February, June, September, December

Susceptible health areas: The Blood, Descending Colon, Excess Strain to Nervous System, Genitals, Liver, Neuritis, Nose, Rectum, Reproductive Organs, Sciatica, Skin, Sometimes the Back, Throat, Urethra

OCTOBER 31   SCORPIO

Age for health changes: 4, 13, 22, 31, 40, 49, 58, 67, 76, 85

Months to guard health: January, February, July, August, September

Susceptible health areas: Anemia, Back and Neck Pains, the Blood, Cramps and Spasms, Descending Colon, Genitals, Melancholia, Mental Disorders,Nose, Palpitations, Rectum, Reproductive Organs, Sometimes the Back, Sudden Nervous Breakdowns, Urethra

Health Cycles for November Birthdays

NOVEMBER 1
Age for health changes:
Months to guard health:
Susceptible health areas:

SCORPIO
1, 10, 19, 28, 37, 46, 55, 64, 73, 82
January, October, December
The Blood, Descending Colon, Eye Problems, Genitals, Headaches, Heart and Circulatory System, High Blood Pressure, Nose, Palpitations, Rectum, Reproductive Organs, Sometimes the Back, Urethra

NOVEMBER 2
Age for health changes:
Months to guard health:
Susceptible health areas:

SCORPIO
2, 11, 20, 29, 38, 47, 56, 65, 74, 83
January, February, July
The Blood, Breasts, Descending Colon, Digestive System Disorders, Genitals, Lymphatic System Disorders, Nose, Ovaries, Rectum, Reproductive Organs, Sometimes the Back, Stomach, Sympathetic Nervous System, Synovial Fluids, Urethra

NOVEMBER 3
Age for health changes:
Months to guard health:
Susceptible health areas:

SCORPIO
3, 12, 21, 30, 39, 48, 57, 66, 75, 84
February, June, September, December
The Blood, Descending Colon, Excess Strain to Nervous System, Genitals, Liver, Neuritis, Nose, Rectum, Reproductive Organs, Sciatica, Skin, Sometimes the Back, Throat, Urethra

NOVEMBER 4
Age for health changes:
Months to guard health:
Susceptible health areas:

SCORPIO
4, 13, 22, 31, 40, 49, 58, 67, 76, 85
January, February, July, August, September
Anemia, Back and Neck Pains, the Blood, Cramps and Spasms, Descending Colon, Genitals, Melancholia, Mental Disorders,Nose, Palpitations, Rectum, Reproductive Organs, Sometimes the Back, Sudden Nervous Breakdowns, Urethra

NOVEMBER 5
Age for health changes:
Months to guard health:
Susceptible health areas:

SCORPIO
5, 14, 23, 32, 41, 50, 59, 68, 77, 86
June, September, December
All Sense, Perception and Sensory Organs, the Blood, Central Nervous System, Descending Colon, Genitals, Insomnia, Nose, Rectum, Reproductive Organs, Respiratory System, Sometimes the Back, Thyroid, Urethra

NOVEMBER 6
Age for health changes:
Months to guard health:
Susceptible health areas:

SCORPIO
6, 15, 24, 33, 42, 51, 60, 69, 78, 87
June, October, November
The Blood, Descending Colon, Genitals, Kidneys, Liver, Lumbar Region Disorders, Nose, Parathyroid, Rectum, Reproductive Organs, Sometimes the Back, Throat, Urethra, Veinous Circulation

NOVEMBER 7
Age for health changes:

SCORPIO
7, 16, 25, 34, 43, 52, 61, 70, 79, 88

| Months to guard health: | January, February, July, August |
| Susceptible health areas: | The Blood, Depression Caused by Mental Stress, Descending Colon, Genitals, Nose, Prone to Drug and Alcohol or Addiction, Rectum, Reproductive Organs, Sensitive Skin Conditions, Sometimes the Back, Urethra |

NOVEMBER 8

	SCORPIO
Age for health changes:	8, 17, 26, 35, 44, 53, 62, 71, 80, 89
Months to guard health:	January, February, July, December
Susceptible health areas:	The Blood, Descending Colon, Headaches, Gall Bladder, Genitals, Intestines, Liver Bile, Nose, Rectum, Reproductive Organs, Rheumatism, Skeletal system, Skin, Spleen, Sometimes the Back, Teeth, Urethra

NOVEMBER 9

	SCORPIO
Age for health changes:	9, 18, 27, 36, 45, 54, 63, 72, 81
Months to guard health:	April, June, October, November
Susceptible health areas:	Contagious Diseases, Chicken Pox, Descending Colon, Genitals, Kidneys, Measles, Muscular System, Nose, Rectum, Red Corpuscles of the Blood, Reproductive Organs, Sometimes the Back, Urethra

NOVEMBER 10

	SCORPIO
Age for health changes:	1, 10, 19, 28, 37, 46, 55, 64, 73, 82
Months to guard health:	January, October, December

Susceptible health areas:	The Blood, Descending Colon, Eye Problems, Genitals, Headaches, Heart and Circulatory System, High Blood Pressure, Nose, Palpitations, Rectum, Reproductive Organs, Sometimes the Back, Urethra

NOVEMBER 11   SCORPIO
Age for health changes: 2, 11, 20, 29, 38, 47, 56, 65, 74, 83
Months to guard health: January, February, July
Susceptible health areas: The Blood, Breasts, Descending Colon, Digestive System Disorders, Genitals, Lymphatic System Disorders, Nose, Ovaries, Rectum, Reproductive Organs, Sometimes the Back, Stomach, Sympathetic Nervous System, Synovial Fluids, Urethra

NOVEMBER 12   SCORPIO
Age for health changes: 3, 12, 21, 30, 39, 48, 57, 66, 75, 84
Months to guard health: February, June, September, December
Susceptible health areas: The Blood, Descending Colon, Excess Strain to Nervous System, Genitals, Liver, Neuritis, Nose, Rectum, Reproductive Organs, Sciatica, Skin, Sometimes the Back, Throat, Urethra

NOVEMBER 13   SCORPIO
Age for health changes: 4, 13, 22, 31, 40, 49, 58, 67, 76, 85
Months to guard health: January, February, July, August, September
Susceptible health areas: Anemia, Back and Neck Pains, the Blood, Cramps and Spasms, Descending Colon, Genitals, Melancholia, Mental Disorders,

Nose, Palpitations, Rectum, Reproductive Organs, Sometimes the Back, Sudden Nervous Breakdowns, Urethra

NOVEMBER 14
Age for health changes:
Months to guard health:
Susceptible health areas:

SCORPIO
5, 14, 23, 32, 41, 50, 59, 68, 77, 86
June, September, December
All Sense, Perception and Sensory Organs, the Blood, Central Nervous System, Descending Colon, Genitals, Insomnia, Nose, Rectum, Reproductive Organs, Respiratory System, Sometimes the Back, Thyroid, Urethra

NOVEMBER 15
Age for health changes:
Months to guard health:
Susceptible health areas:

SCORPIO
6, 15, 24, 33, 42, 51, 60, 69, 78, 87
June, October, November
The Blood, Descending Colon, Genitals, Kidneys, Liver, Lumbar Region Disorders, Nose, Parathyroid, Rectum, Reproductive Organs, Sometimes the Back, Throat, Urethra, Veinous Circulation

NOVEMBER 16
Age for health changes:
Months to guard health:
Susceptible health areas:

SCORPIO
7, 16, 25, 34, 43, 52, 61, 70, 79, 88
January, February, July, August
The Blood, Depression Caused by Mental Stress, Descending Colon, Genitals, Nose, Prone to Drug and Alcohol or Addiction, Rectum, Reproductive Organs, Sensitive Skin Conditions, Sometimes the Back, Urethra

NOVEMBER 17

SCORPIO

Age for health changes:
8, 17, 26, 35, 44, 53, 62, 71, 80, 89

Months to guard health:
January, February, July, December

Susceptible health areas:
The Blood, Descending Colon, Headaches, Gall Bladder, Genitals, Intestines, Liver Bile, Nose, Rectum, Reproductive Organs, Rheumatism, Skeletal system, Skin, Spleen, Sometimes the Back, Teeth, Urethra

NOVEMBER 18

SCORPIO

Age for health changes:
9, 18, 27, 36, 45, 54, 63, 72, 81

Months to guard health:
April, June, October, November

Susceptible health areas:
Contagious Diseases, Chicken Pox, Descending Colon, Genitals, Kidneys, Measles, Muscular System, Nose, Rectum, Red Corpuscles of the Blood, Reproductive Organs, Sometimes the Back, Urethra

NOVEMBER 19

SCORPIO

Age for health changes:
1, 10, 19, 28, 37, 46, 55, 64, 73, 82

Months to guard health:
January, October, December

Susceptible health areas:
The Blood, Descending Colon, Eye Problems, Genitals, Headaches, Heart and Circulatory System, High Blood Pressure, Nose, Palpitations, Rectum, Reproductive Organs, Sometimes the Back, Urethra

NOVEMBER 20

SCORPIO

Age for health changes:
2, 11, 20, 29, 38, 47, 56, 65, 74, 83

Months to guard health: January, February, July
Susceptible health areas: The Blood, Breasts, Descending Colon, Digestive System Disorders, Genitals, Lymphatic System Disorders, Nose, Ovaries, Rectum, Reproductive Organs, Sometimes the Back, Stomach, Sympathetic Nervous System, Synovial Fluids, Urethra

NOVEMBER 21   SCORPIO
Age for health changes: 3, 12, 21, 30, 39, 48, 57, 66, 75, 84
Months to guard health: February, June, September, December
Susceptible health areas: The Blood, Descending Colon, Excess Strain to Nervous System, Genitals, Liver, Neuritis, Nose, Rectum, Reproductive Organs, Sciatica, Skin, Sometimes the Back, Throat, Urethra

NOVEMBER 22   SAGITTARIUS
Age for health changes: 4, 13, 22, 31, 40, 49, 58, 67, 76, 85
Months to guard health: January, February, July, August, September
Susceptible health areas: Anemia, Cramps and Spasms, Back and Neck Pains, Femur Bone, Hips, Liver, Melancholia, Mental Disorders, Sudden Nervous Breakdowns, Sacral Region, Thighs, Veins

NOVEMBER 23   SAGITTARIUS
Age for health changes: 5, 14, 23, 32, 41, 50, 59, 68, 77, 86
Months to guard health: June, September, December
Susceptible health areas: All Sense, Perception and Sensory Organs, Central Nervous System, Femur Bone,

Hips, Insomnia, Liver, Respiratory System, Sacral Region, Thighs, Thyroid, Veins

NOVEMBER 24
Age for health changes:
Months to guard health:
Susceptible health areas:

SAGITTARIUS
6, 15, 24, 33, 42, 51, 60, 69, 78, 87
June, October, November
Femur Bone, Hips, Kidneys, Liver, Lumbar Region Disorders, Parathyroid, Sacral Region, Thighs, Throat, Veins, Veinous Circulation

NOVEMBER 25
Age for health changes:
Months to guard health:
Susceptible health areas:

SAGITTARIUS
7, 16, 25, 34, 43, 52, 61, 70, 79, 88
January, February, July, August
Depression Caused by Mental Stress, Femur Bone, Hips, Liver, Prone to Drug or Alcohol Addiction, Sacral Region, Sensitive Skin Conditions, Thighs, Veins

NOVEMBER 26
Age for health changes:
Months to guard health:
Susceptible health areas:

SAGITTARIUS
8, 17, 26, 35, 44, 53, 62, 71, 80, 89
January, February, July, December
Femur Bone, Gall Bladder, Headaches, Hips, Intestines, Liver, Liver Bile, Rheumatism, Sacral Region, Skeletal System, Skin, Spleen, Teeth, Thighs, Veins

NOVEMBER 27
Age for health changes:
Months to guard health:

SAGITTARIUS
9, 18, 27, 36, 45, 54, 63, 72, 81
April, June, October, November

Susceptible health areas:	Chicken Pox, Contagious Diseases, Femur Bone, Hips, Kidneys, Liver, Measles, Muscular System, Red Corpuscles of the Blood, Sacral Region, Thighs, Veins

NOVEMBER 28   SAGITTARIUS
Age for health changes: 1, 10, 19, 28, 37, 46, 55, 64, 73, 82
Months to guard health: January, October, December
Susceptible health areas: Eye Problems, Femur Bone, Headaches, Heart and Circulatory System, High Blood Pressure, Hips, Liver, Palpitations, Sacral Region, Thighs, Veins

NOVEMBER 29   SAGITTARIUS
Age for health changes: 2, 11, 20, 29, 38, 47, 56, 65, 74, 83
Months to guard health: January, February, July
Susceptible health areas: Breasts, Digestive System Disorders, Femur Bone, Hips, Lymphatic System Disorders, Liver, Ovaries, Sacral Region, Stomach, Sympathetic Nervous System, Synovial Fluids, Thighs, Veins

NOVEMBER 30   SAGITTARIUS
Age for health changes: 3, 12, 21, 30, 39, 48, 57, 66, 75, 84
Months to guard health: February, June, September, December
Susceptible health areas: Excess Strain to Nervous System, Femur Bone, Hips, Liver, Neuritis, Sacral Region, Sciatica, Skin, Thighs, Throat, Veins

Health Cycles for December Birthdays

DECEMBER 1
Age for health changes:
Months to guard health:
Susceptible health areas:

SAGITTARIUS
1, 10, 19, 28, 37, 46, 55, 64, 73, 82
January, October, December
Eye Problems, Femur Bone, Headaches, Heart and Circulatory System, High Blood Pressure, Hips, Liver, Palpitations, Sacral Region, Thighs, Veins

DECEMBER 2
Age for health changes:
Months to guard health:
Susceptible health areas:

SAGITTARIUS
2, 11, 20, 29, 38, 47, 56, 65, 74, 83
January, February, July
Breasts, Digestive System Disorders, Femur Bone, Hips, Lymphatic System Disorders, Liver, Ovaries, Sacral Region, Stomach, Sympathetic Nervous System, Synovial Fluids, Thighs, Veins

DECEMBER 3
Age for health changes:
Months to guard health:
Susceptible health areas:

SAGITTARIUS
3, 12, 21, 30, 39, 48, 57, 66, 75, 84
February, June, September, December
Excess Strain to Nervous System, Femur Bone, Hips, Liver, Neuritis, Sacral Region, Sciatica, Skin, Thighs, Throat, Veins

DECEMBER 4
Age for health changes:
Months to guard health:
Susceptible health areas:

SAGITTARIUS
4, 13, 22, 31, 40, 49, 58, 67, 76, 85
January, February, July, August, September
Anemia, Cramps and Spasms, Back and Neck Pains, Femur Bone, Hips, Liver,

Melancholia, Mental Disorders, Sudden
Nervous Breakdowns, Sacral Region,
Thighs, Veins

DECEMBER 5   SAGITTARIUS
Age for health changes: 5, 14, 23, 32, 41, 50, 59, 68, 77, 86
Months to guard health: June, September, December
Susceptible health areas: All Sense, Perception and Sensory Organs,
                                    Central Nervous System, Femur Bone,
                                    Hips, Insomnia, Liver, Respiratory System,
                                    Sacral Region, Thighs, Thyroid, Veins

DECEMBER 6   SAGITTARIUS
Age for health changes: 6, 15, 24, 33, 42, 51, 60, 69, 78, 87
Months to guard health: June, October, November
Susceptible health areas: Femur Bone, Hips, Kidneys, Liver,
                                    Lumbar Region Disorders, Parathyroid,
                                    Sacral Region, Thighs, Throat, Veins,
                                    Veinous Circulation

DECEMBER 7   SAGITTARIUS
Age for health changes: 7, 16, 25, 34, 43, 52, 61, 70, 79, 88
Months to guard health: January, February, July, August
Susceptible health areas: Depression Caused by Mental Stress,
                                    Femur Bone, Hips, Liver, Prone to Drug
                                    or Alcohol Addiction, Sacral Region,
                                    Sensitive Skin Conditions, Thighs, Veins

DECEMBER 8   SAGITTARIUS
Age for health changes: 8, 17, 26, 35, 44, 53, 62, 71, 80, 89
Months to guard health: January, February, July, December

Susceptible health areas: Femur Bone, Gall Bladder, Headaches, Hips, Intestines, Liver, Liver Bile, Rheumatism, Sacral Region, Skeletal System, Skin, Spleen, Teeth, Thighs, Veins

DECEMBER 9 SAGITTARIUS
Age for health changes: 9, 18, 27, 36, 45, 54, 63, 72, 81
Months to guard health: April, June, October, November
Susceptible health areas: Chicken Pox, Contagious Diseases, Femur Bone, Hips, Kidneys, Liver, Measles, Muscular System, Red Corpuscles of the Blood, Sacral Region, Thighs, Veins

DECEMBER 10 SAGITTARIUS
Age for health changes: 1, 10, 19, 28, 37, 46, 55, 64, 73, 82
Months to guard health: January, October, December
Susceptible health areas: Eye Problems, Femur Bone, Headaches, Heart and Circulatory System, High Blood Pressure, Hips, Liver, Palpitations, Sacral Region, Thighs, Veins

DECEMBER 11 SAGITTARIUS
Age for health changes: 2, 11, 20, 29, 38, 47, 56, 65, 74, 83
Months to guard health: January, February, July
Susceptible health areas: Breasts, Digestive System Disorders, Femur Bone, Hips, Lymphatic System Disorders, Liver, Ovaries, Sacral Region, Stomach, Sympathetic Nervous System, Synovial Fluids, Thighs, Veins

DECEMBER 12 SAGITTARIUS
Age for health changes: 3, 12, 21, 30, 39, 48, 57, 66, 75, 84

Months to guard health: February, June, September, December
Susceptible health areas: Excess Strain to Nervous System, Femur
                                 Bone, Hips, Liver, Neuritis, Sacral Region,
                                 Sciatica, Skin, Thighs, Throat, Veins

DECEMBER 13   SAGITTARIUS
Age for health changes: 4, 13, 22, 31, 40, 49, 58, 67, 76, 85
Months to guard health: January, February, July, August, September
Susceptible health areas: Anemia, Cramps and Spasms, Back and
                                 Neck Pains, Femur Bone, Hips, Liver,
                                 Melancholia, Mental Disorders, Sudden
                                 Nervous Breakdowns, Sacral Region,
                                 Thighs, Veins

DECEMBER 14   SAGITTARIUS
Age for health changes: 5, 14, 23, 32, 41, 50, 59, 68, 77, 86
Months to guard health: June, September, December
Susceptible health areas: All Sense, Perception and Sensory Organs,
                                 Central Nervous System, Femur Bone,
                                 Hips, Insomnia, Liver, Respiratory System,
                                 Sacral Region, Thighs, Thyroid, Veins

DECEMBER 15   SAGITTARIUS
Age for health changes: 6, 15, 24, 33, 42, 51, 60, 69, 78, 87
Months to guard health: June, October, November
Susceptible health areas: Femur Bone, Hips, Kidneys, Liver,
                                 Lumbar Region Disorders, Parathyroid,
                                 Sacral Region, Thighs, Throat, Veins,
                                 Veinous Circulation

DECEMBER 16   SAGITTARIUS
Age for health changes: 7, 16, 25, 34, 43, 52, 61, 70, 79, 88

Months to guard health: January, February, July, August
Susceptible health areas: Depression Caused by Mental Stress, Femur Bone, Hips, Liver, Prone to Drug or Alcohol Addiction, Sacral Region, Sensitive Skin Conditions, Thighs, Veins

DECEMBER 17 SAGITTARIUS
Age for health changes: 8, 17, 26, 35, 44, 53, 62, 71, 80, 89
Months to guard health: January, February, July, December
Susceptible health areas: Femur Bone, Gall Bladder, Headaches, Hips, Intestines, Liver, Liver Bile, Rheumatism, Sacral Region, Skeletal System, Skin, Spleen, Teeth, Thighs, Veins

DECEMBER 18 SAGITTARIUS
Age for health changes: 9, 18, 27, 36, 45, 54, 63, 72, 81
Months to guard health: April, June, October, November
Susceptible health areas: Chicken Pox, Contagious Diseases, Femur Bone, Hips, Kidneys, Liver, Measles, Muscular System, Red Corpuscles of the Blood, Sacral Region, Thighs, Veins

DECEMBER 19 SAGITTARIUS
Age for health changes: 1, 10, 19, 28, 37, 46, 55, 64, 73, 82
Months to guard health: January, October, December
Susceptible health areas: Eye Problems, Femur Bone, Headaches, Heart and Circulatory System, High Blood Pressure, Hips, Liver, Palpitations, Sacral Region, Thighs, Veins

DECEMBER 20 SAGITTARIUS
Age for health changes: 2, 11, 20, 29, 38, 47, 56, 65, 74, 83

Months to guard health: January, February, July
Susceptible health areas: Breasts, Digestive System Disorders, Femur Bone, Hips, Lymphatic System Disorders, Liver, Ovaries, Sacral Region, Stomach, Sympathetic Nervous System, Synovial Fluids, Thighs, Veins

DECEMBER 21   SAGITTARIUS
Age for health changes: 3, 12, 21, 30, 39, 48, 57, 66, 75, 84
Months to guard health: February, June, September, December
Susceptible health areas: Excess Strain to Nervous System, Femur Bone, Hips, Liver, Neuritis, Sacral Region, Sciatica, Skin, Thighs, Throat, Veins

DECEMBER 22   CAPRICORN
Age for health changes: 4, 13, 22, 31, 40, 49, 58, 67, 76, 85
Month to guard health: January, February, July, August, September
Susceptible health areas: Anemia, Bones, Back and Neck Pains, Cramps and Spasms, Kneecaps, Melancholia, Mental Disorders, Palpitations, Skin, Sudden Nervous Breakdowns, Teeth

DECEMBER 23   CAPRICORN
Age for health changes: 5, 14, 23, 32, 41, 50, 59, 68, 77, 86
Month to guard health: June, September, December
Susceptible health areas: All Sense, Perception and Sensory Organs, Bones, Central Nervous System, Insomnia, Kneecaps, Respiratory System, Skin, Teeth, Thyroid

DECEMBER 24   CAPRICORN
Age for health changes: 6, 15, 24, 33, 42, 51, 60, 69, 78, 87

Month to guard health: May, October, November
Susceptible health areas: Bones, Kidneys, Kneecaps, Liver, Lumbar Region Disorders, Parathyroid, Teeth, Throat, Skin, Veinous Circulation

DECEMBER 25   CAPRICORN
Age for health changes: 7, 16, 25, 34, 43, 52, 61, 70, 79, 88
Month to guard health: January, February, July, August
Susceptible health areas: Bones, Depression from Mental Stress, Kneecaps, Prone to Drug and Alcohol Addiction, Sensitive Skin Conditions, Teeth

DECEMBER 26   CAPRICORN
Age for health changes: 8, 17, 26, 35, 44, 53, 62, 71, 80
Month to guard health: January, February, July, December
Susceptible health areas: Bones, Gall Bladder, Headaches, Intestines, Kneecaps, Liver Bile, Rheumatism, Skeletal System, Skin, Spleen, Teeth

DECEMBER 27   CAPRICORN
Age for health changes: 9, 18, 27, 36, 45, 54, 63, 72, 81
Month to guard health: April, May, October, November
Susceptible health areas: Bones, Chicken Pox, Contagious Diseases, Kidneys, Kneecaps, Measles, Muscular System, Red Corpuscles of the Blood, Skin, Teeth

DECEMBER 28   CAPRICORN
Age for health changes: 1, 10, 19, 28, 37, 46, 55, 64, 73, 82
Months to guard health: January, October, December
Susceptible health areas: Bones, Eye Problems, Headaches, Heart and Circulatory System, High Blood Pressure, Kneecaps, Palpitations, Skin, Teeth

DECEMBER 29

Age for health changes:
Month to guard health:
Susceptible health areas:

CAPRICORN

2, 11, 20, 29, 38, 47, 56, 65, 74, 83
January, February, July
Bones, Breasts, Digestive system Disorders, Kneecaps, Lymphatic System Disorders, Ovaries, Skin, Stomach, Sympathetic Nervous System, Synovial Fluids, Teeth

DECEMBER 30

Age for health changes:
Month to guard health:
Susceptible health areas:

CAPRICORN

3, 12, 21, 30, 39, 48, 57, 66, 75, 84
February, June, September, December
Bones, Excess Strain to Nervous System, Kneecaps, Liver, Neuritis, Sciatica, Skin, Teeth, Throat

DECEMBER 31

Age for health changes:
Month to guard health:
Susceptible health areas:

CAPRICORN

4, 13, 22, 31, 40, 49, 58, 67, 76, 85
January, February, July, August, September
Anemia, Bones, Back and Neck Pains, Cramps and Spasms, Kneecaps, Melancholia, Mental Disorders, Palpitations, Skin, Sudden Nervous Breakdowns, Teeth

Passport to the Moon

Passport to the Moon

Emotions have long been portrayed in terms of the sea. Mood swings, instinct and sensitivity indicate how we feel about things and how our feelings affect others. By observing the waxing and waning phases of the moon, you can create opportunity to energize the life you desire. Learn to surf the cycles of the moon and enjoy your own natural rhythms.

Our bodies are made up of over 70 percent water and our biorhythms magnetically react like micro-oceans to the lunar cycles, personalized by the phase, sign and degree of the moon. Tracking this monthly journey through the ebb and flow acts like a personal emotional barometer setting the tone for our daily lives. The moon rules the tides and is a powerful ruler over human emotion.

As you learn to surf the cycles of the moon you will develop an understanding of your lunar nature. Keep your life in sync by observing the rise and fall of your emotional cycles. Treasure seekers can soar the emotional heights or plummet into the emotional depths, while discerning balance to assure a smooth ride.

Test the waters by keeping a journal or jot down notes on your calendar. Check out the timing of each new moon and astrological sign. Then consider the keywords for each sign of the zodiac. By energizing your dreams on the new moon you will catch the crest of the wave to create your vision and pursue your goals. By the full moon you will witness the progress of your vision. When you reach the waning cycle you can use your treasure chest of wisdom to decide how to proceed with the next turn of the tide. Moon cycles offer a sense of direction for all areas of life.

New Moon Date & Sign		Full Moon Date & Sign	
10-06-2002	Libra	10-21-2002	Aries
11-04-2002	Scorpio	11-20-2002	Taurus
12-04-2002	Sagittarius	12-19-2002	Gemini
1-02-2003	Capricorn	1-18-2003	Cancer
2-01-2003	Aquarius	2-16-2003	Leo
3-03-2003	Pisces	3-18-2003	Virgo
4-01-2003	Aries	4-16-2003	Libra
5-01-2003	Taurus	5-16-2003	Scorpio
5-31-2003	Gemini	6-14-2003	Sagittarius
6-29-2003	Cancer	7-13-2003	Capricorn
7-29-2003	Leo	8-12-2003	Aquarius
8-27-2003	Virgo	9-10-2003	Pisces
9-26-2003	Libra	10-10-2003	Aries
10-25-2003	Scorpio	11-09-2003	Taurus
11-23-2003	Sagittarius	12-08-2003	Gemini
For dates beyond 2003, consult a calendar or Llewellyn's Moon Sign book published annually			

Aries Moon—Anchors away! Take a chance and go for it. Don't become impatient and don't burn your bridges behind you.

Taurus Moon—Be determined and remain practical in business affairs. Enjoy making money. Indulge yourself and your love interest by dining at the Captain's table or order a gourmet snack.

Gemini Moon—If you're bored by routine, socialize. With your lightening thoughts, quick wit and gift of gab you'll be a whirlwind. Gemini is the sign of the twins, so you may be working on two projects at once.

Cancer Moon—Share your wonderful natural talents of nurturing and caring with the rest of the world. Don't act like a hermit and stay on deck. Come ashore!

Leo Moon—Avoid risking your worldly goods in an attempt to be generous. You will be tempted to be the life of the party. Public relations and networking go a long way to enhance a business deal.

Virgo Moon—Remember that you're needs are just as important as the needs of others. Think about yourself, too, as you analyze and plan your goals. Keep those medical appointments at Sick Bay. Try not to worry so much. Lighten up!

Libra Moon—Share your love of beauty from art, music and literature. Dance under the stars. Consider joining a social group with your favorite mate. Practice diplomacy and avoid procrastination with coworkers and shipmates.

Scorpio Moon—Still waters run deep. Emotions will be intense. You may feel secretive and suspicious. Your loyalty is strong once a commitment is made. Trust your instincts. Your investigative skills will be top notch.

Sagittarius Moon—You might consider relocating to a distant location. You feel the spirit of adventure flow through your veins and don't mind the feeling of being fancy-free.

Capricorn Moon—Public opinion will keep you alert and cautious. Keep a sense of humor in all your daily affairs, but don't risk your public image.

Aquarius Moon—Your humanitarian heart will want to save the whales. All kinds of creative ideas will flow with ease. With your eyes on the future, don't forget to appreciate the here and now.

Pisces Moon—Watch your dreams for solutions to obstacles that you have been facing. Don't choose to be a victim of circumstance. Face emotional hurts and disappointments. Replace foggy thoughts with spiritual concepts. Take a risk on reality.

Sun Signs

Personality Traits
and
Compatibilities

Table 34. Sun Sign Personality Traits

ARIES (The Ram)		March 21 to April 19		(Cardinal Fire)
Me first	Pioneers	Leaders	Assertive	Active
Versatile	Impatient	Impulsive	Courageous	Initiative
Temper	Self-willed	Brusque	Urgent	No grudges

TAURUS (The Bull)		April 20 to May 20		(Fixed Earth)
Stubborn	Determined	Practical	Conventional	Security
Endurance	Money Making	Loves Luxury	Thorough	Collectors
Laziness	Jealous	Reliable	Possessive	Loves Beauty

GEMINI (The Twins)		May 21 to June 21		(Mutable Air)
Talkative	Versatile	Alert	Impulsive	Adaptable
Restless	Fast talkers	Salesmen	Changeable	Curiosity
Nervous	Unreliable	Moody	Mentally quick	Bored by routine

CANCER (The Crab)		June 22 to July 22		(Cardinal Water)
Emotional	Changeable	Moody	Indirect	Evasive
Conventional	Home loving	Tenacious	Sympathetic	Kind
Contrary	Clannish	Psychic	Security	Maternal

LEO (The Lion)		July 23 to August 22		(Fixed Fire)
Creative	Dramatic	Strong ego	Actor/Actress	Children
Gambler	Affectionate	Loyal	Noble	Vain
Arrogant	Born leader	Proud	Generous	Fraternal

VIRGO (The Virgin)		August 23 to September 22		(Mutable Air)
Analytical	Critical	Organizer	Work/health	Worrier
Methodical	Perfectionist	Medicine	Intelligence	Secretive
Efficiency	Narrow-minded	Therapists	Perfectionist	Smug

LIBRA (The Scales)		September 23 to October 22		(Cardinal Air)
Balance	Justice	Peace maker	Vacillates	Loves beauty
Charm	Diplomacy	Sociable	Partnerships	Law/Lawyers
Secrecy	Suave	Arbitrary	Procrastinates	Artistic

SCORPIO (The Scorpion)		October 23 to November 21		(Fixed Water)
Intense	Secretive	Sexual	Investigate	Opinionated
Loyal	Possessive	Jealous	Vindictive	Temper
Passionate	Persistent	Holds grudge	Ruthless	Daring

SAGITTARIUS (The Archer)		November 22 to December 21		(Mutable Fire)
Languages	Athletic	Education	Honest	Blunt
Gambler	Rebel	Restless	Jovial	Optimistic
Travel	Foreigners	Prophetic	Religion	Philosophical

CAPRICORN (The Goat)		December 22 to January 19		(Cardinal Earth)
Patient	Ambitious	Political	Cautious	Thoughtful
Tolerance	Conventional	Suspicious	Resentful	Worrier
Unforgiving	Teacher	Pessimistic	Conceit	Responsible

AQUARIUS (The Water Bearer)		January 20 to February 18		(Fixed Air)
Detached	Original	Inventive	Unorthodox	Unconventional
Friendship	Groups	Democratic	Rebellious	Destroys
Erratic	Humanitarian	Progressive	Therapist	Intuition

PISCES (The Fishes)		February 19 to March 20		(Mutable Water)
Psychic	Idealistic	Sensitive	Indecisive	Compassionate
Neglectful	Indifferent	Dancer	Poet/Artist	Prisons
Martyrs	Psychiatrist	Psychologist	Self-sacrificing	Spiritual

Fixed Signs:

Fixed signs are usually not open to change, but they know who they are and what they want. They are very self-assured and often rebellious and succeed through perseverance. Fixed signs are often loners.

Mutable Signs:

Mutable signs are very flexible and adaptable and love variety and change. They don't like to be tied down and love to travel. Mutable signs are easily bored and demand lots of excitement.

Cardinal Signs:

Cardinal signs are go-getters and get things started (business, family, groups, etc.), and they focus on one thing at a time. Cardinals are usually "movers and shakers" and are usually leaders and pioneers in their field of endeavor.

Table 35. Sun Sign Compatibility Chart

Astrological Sign	Best Compatibility	Good Compatibility
ARIES	Aries Leo Sagittarius	Gemini Libra Aquarius
TAURUS	Taurus Virgo Capricorn	Cancer Scorpio Pisces
GEMINI	Gemini Libra Aquarius	Aries Leo Sagittarius
CANCER	Cancer Scorpio Pisces	Taurus Virgo Capricorn
LEO	Leo Aries Sagittarius	Gemini Libra Aquarius
VIRGO	Virgo Capricorn Taurus	Cancer Scorpio Pisces
LIBRA	Libra Gemini Aquarius	Aries Leo Sagittarius
SCORPIO	Scorpio Pisces Capricorn	Taurus Virgo Capricorn
SAGITTARIUS	Sagittarius Leo Aries	Gemini Libra Aquarius
CAPRICORN	Capricorn Taurus Virgo	Cancer Scorpio Pisces
AQUARIUS	Aquarius Gemini Libra	Aries Leo Sagittarius
PISCES	Pisces Cancer Scorpio	Taurus Virgo Capricorn

Star Tips for Luck

Lucky Numbers
Lucky Days
What's in a Phone Number?

Lucky Numbers

Now you don't have to pick your lucky numbers using the "eeny-meeny-miney-mo" technique. Ancient manuscripts reveal the technique used to calculate your six personal lucky numbers and the lucky days to play them.

1<u>st</u> <u>Lucky Number</u> is calculated by numerically translating the name of each zodiac sign.

2<u>nd</u> & 3<u>rd</u> <u>Lucky Numbers</u> are determined by astrology. Since antiquity, each sign has had its own specific number assignment.

4<u>th</u> <u>Lucky Number</u> is derived from the Hebraic Cabal. When this alphabet was compiled, all the specific characteristics attributed to each sign were taken into consideration.

5<u>th</u> <u>Lucky Number</u>—The ancient Greeks attributed twelve gods from their mythology to the twelve signs of the zodiac. These Greek gods are considered to have a positive influence on their respective signs. Their names have been translated numerologically.

6<u>th</u> <u>Lucky Number</u> corresponds to the letter of the Hebraic alphabet, which was attributed to each sign in the beginning of time. This letter is translated numerologically. These numbers are particularly lucky for any games of chance.

Table 36. Lucky Numbers

Sun Sign	Lucky Numbers					
Aries	7	11	13	18	22	22/4
Taurus	10	4	2	20	51	23
Gemini	12	9	16	34	26	24
Cancer	8	4	7	15	32	13
Leo	5	1	10	14	17	19
Virgo	8	6	13	12	34	8
Libra	6	9	4	10	55	23
Scorpio	5	8	34	18	16	6
Sagittarius	9	9	16	6	32	23
Capricorn	7	5	14	9	26	19
Aquarius	8	4	9	3	23	19
Pisces	8	3	7	1	43	23

Lucky Days

Lucky days are determined by calculating the influence of the planets on each sign of the zodiac. Here are those days for each of the signs. Fortune smiles on these days and numbers, whenever you play any prize-winning game, or whenever you have an important decision to make.

Table 37. Lucky Days

SUN SIGN	INFLUENCED BY		
	Planet	Day	No.
ARIES	Saturn	Saturday	1
	Mercury	Wednesday	5
TAURUS	Venus	Friday	3
	Moon	Monday	2
GEMINI	Mercury	Wednesday	5
	Sun	Sunday	7
CANCER	Moon	Monday	2
	Jupiter	Thursday	4
LEO	Sun	Sunday	7
	Mars	Tuesday	6
VIRGO	Mercury	Wednesday	5
	Sun	Sunday	7
LIBRA	Venus	Friday	3
	Saturn	Saturday	1
SCORPIO	Mars	Tuesday	6
	Sun	Sunday	7
SAGITTARIUS	Jupiter	Thursday	4
	Moon	Monday	2
CAPRICORN	Saturn	Saturday	1
	Mars	Tuesday	6
AQUARIUS	Saturn	Saturday	1
	Mercury	Wednesday	5
PISCES	Jupiter	Thursday	4
	Venus	Friday	3

What's in a Phone Number?

The ancient science of numerology is defined by Webster as "the study of the hidden significance of numbers and letters". Every word or name vibrates to a number and every number has its own specific meaning. Since all numbers have power and energy, why not consider the numerical secrets of your phone number.

To calculate your phone number, add each digit together and reduce to a single digit. Do not use your area code. For example, let's add the phone number for calling information:

$$555\text{-}1212 = 5 + 5 + 5 + 1 + 2 + 1 + 2 = 21 = 3$$

(In numerology, the number 3 represents communication)

Calculate your phone number and check below to see the type of calls you can expect to get.

1

People who call this number will want to talk to you—not a machine—and will want to give you ALL the details about everything. It's hard to stick to just ONE subject. And watch out for misunderstandings caused by unusual breakdowns in communication.

2

This number attracts in-depth conversations and lots of secrets, but you may find yourself being put on hold while you "hurry up and wait." You'll definitely learn cooperation and patience with this phone number.

3

This is a great number for communication and will attract lots of social invitations, important dates, good news, and lots of surprises! However, don't allow gossip to turn negative—harsh words can be heartbreaking.

4

No short messages with this number, and you can get a lot done on this phone—it's good for getting to the root of matters. This phone number could bring calls that interrupt your busy schedule or cause you to feel limited and restricted at times.

5

If you like talking to a lot of different people from all walks of life, you'll love this number. You'll attract lots of calls for lots of different reasons—this can be good or bad, depending on the mood you're in.

6

Let's get serious...might as well, because conversations on this phone will be quite meaningful and more fun than a soap opera. You'll get lots of calls relating to responsibilities associated with home, family and loved ones.

7

Plan to be up on your own personal philosophy with this number, and forget about trying to get a commitment or quick decisions with this vibration. You may also get a lot of calls that surround you in a veil of secrecy and you just may share some secrets of your own as well.

8

People who call will always be in a hurry and some callers may even test your authority. You'll attract lots of solicitors with this number, but will also attract calls offering unexpected opportunities. This is a great number for home-based businesses, as you will attract power and money.

9

You'll love talking to so many people in distant places and getting news from afar, but be prepared to pay for those long distance charges. Expect drama and high intensity from people closer to home, and calls that tie up lots of loose ends.

About the Authors

Gloria Gray
International Spiritual Consultant

Gloria is a highly-skilled intuitive and Spiritual Consultant, whose experience spans 25 years utilizing the ancient arts, such as numerology, astrology and the tarot. She is a charter member of the National Psychic Corporation, Inc.

Gloria was acknowledged as "the world's greatest numerologist" by author Bill Bailey in his 1996 Simon & Schuster book, "America's Good News Almanac." She predicted this book on Bill's birthday, two years before publication. Gloria is also a published author. She contributes spiritual articles to numerous magazines including the "True Spirit" newsletter. Her first book, "Mystic Quest", was published in 1996.

Now retired from a 15 year career in law enforcement as a 911—(police/fire/medical) communications officer in California and Oregon, she makes her home in Central California. During her career in California she was the third female to be accepted into the Galt Lion's Club where she was elected to serve on the Board of Directors. While living and working in Oregon she also served on the Board of Directors for the Siuslaw Area Women's Center in Florence, Oregon where she counseled victims of domestic violence. She currently serves on the Board of Directors for the Lodi Writers Association.

We are all here to learn, to teach, and to help one another. Gloria offers group/individual classes and spiritual workshops in the Great Northwest and Canada. You can contact Gloria at Gloria@truespiritnews.com for her current workshop and speaking schedule.

Jenni Sinclair
Clairsentient and Spiritual Consultant

Jenni is an internationally known clairsentient and spiritual consultant whose in-depth readings will illuminate your life path and help guide you to your true destiny. Jenni's purpose is to help you gain inner peace, greater confidence, and higher self-esteem by providing guidance and insight concerning relationships, money, career, health and family.

Jenni's experience spans over 25 years covering the areas of Tarot, Hand Reading, Numerology, and Astrology. Having been featured on various television and radio programs nationwide, Jenni has a following of clients internationally who rely on her spiritual counseling regarding the past, present and future.

On the radio, at exclusive in-home parties for corporate and private clients, and for those in the entertainment industry, Jenni consistently astounds believers and skeptics alike with her extraordinary accurate and upbeat readings.

Jenni currently resides in Portland, Oregon with her husband, Don, and her two cats, Pansy and Tama. You can contact Jenni at jenni@true-spiritnews.com for her current workshop and speaking schedule or to arrange for a personal reading.

Bibliography

Cheiro—*Cheiro's* Book of Numbers
    Prentice Hall Press—New York—1964

Cunningham, Scott—*Cunningham's Encyclopedia of Crystal, Gem & Metal Magic*
    Llewellyn Publications—St. Paul, MN—1999

Dodge, Ellin—*Numerology Has Your Number*
    Simon & Schuster—New York—1988

Goodman, Linda—*Linda Goodman's Star Signs*
    St. Martin's Press—New York—1988

Goodwin, Matthew Oliver—*Numerology, The Complete Guide*
    Newcastle Publications—North Hollywood, CA—1981

Hendrickson, Robert—*The Ocean Almanac*
    Doubleday—Garden City, NY—1984

Kunz, George Frederick—*The Curious Lore of Precihous Stones*
    Dover Publications, Inc.—New York—1971

Jordan, Juno—Numerology, *The Romance in Your Name*
    DeVorss & Co.—Marina del Rey, CA—1965

Llewellyn Publications—*Llewellyn's Moon Sign Book and Gardening Almanac*
    Llewellyn Publications—St. Paul, MN—2001

Line, Julia—*The Numerology Workbook*
    Aquarian Press—Great Britain—1985

Oxford—*The Oxford Dictionary of Quotations*
    Oxford University Press—London—1941

Playfair, Guy & Hill, Scott—*The Cycles of Heaven*
    Avon Books—New York—1979

Stein, Sandra Kovacs—*Instant Numerology*
    Newcastle Publishing Company, Inc.—North Hollywood, CA—1986

Stevenson, Burton—*The Home Book of Quotations Classical and Modern*
   Dodd, Mead & Company—New York—1967
Valla, Mary—*The Power of Numbers*
   DeVorss & Co.—Marina del Rey, CA 1971

Log Notes

Log Notes

Log Notes

Log Notes

Log Notes

Log Notes

0-595-24869-1

Printed in the United States
31367LVS00006B/169-186